THE INVISIBLE GAME

MINDSET OF A WINNING TEAM

THE **MENTAL SIDE** OF E**SPORTS**

Zoltan Andrejkovics

#E**SPORTS** #**PROFESSIONAL**GAMING
#**MENTAL**DEVELOPMENT
#**LIFE**LESSONS #**ESPORT**PSYCHOLOGY

ISBN: 1517457017
ISBN-13: 978-1517457013

Book's Website:
www.TheInvisibleGame.com

Author's social media:
Facebook page facebook.com/andzol
Twitter page twitter.com/andzol
LinkedIn page linkedin.com/in/andzol

Fourth edition: September 2017

I believe that gaming is not about
defeating our opponents;
rather, it's about discovering the depth of
our internal greatness.

Dedicated to Gamers.

TABLE OF **CONTENTS**

ACKNOWLEDGEMENT

Special thank you to **Attila Peter Meszaros** and **Csaba Koltai** who translated this book.

Thank you to **Adam Faniszlo** who designed the lovely cover of this book.

Thank you to **Monster Energy**, main partner of this book.

FOREWORD

I was eight years old when I got introduced to the first generation of PC games. I'd consider myself lucky because back then personal computers were quite a rarity in our neighborhood. Most people didn't even know what their purpose was, let alone how to operate them. I'll never forget my summer break that, in its majority, was spent at my grandma's place. Every afternoon my friends and I went to play football (the traditional kind, not the American) at the local pitch where we kicked the ball until we could barely see past our noses in the dark. Then I'd finally run home to my granny's delicious supper, followed by my typically half-hearted attempts to be a good boy and go to sleep – usually with little success.

My uncle, who was a young lad then, normally turned on his brand new computer around this time to load his newest PC game. Naturally, I always snuck over to him to take part in the mission, and after a couple of hours of playing, tired but satisfied by my new experiences, I would finally turn in for the night. My interest in eSports most certainly took root during these secret nocturnal adventures.

Today eSports are more than just simple gaming. I've met countless incredibly talented young people in my life, but only a few can say that they're among the best in the world. As long as we consider eSports merely play of some sort, it will remain as such in our minds. It will only become a sport when we recognize its depth, when, during a contest, we not only try to beat our opponents but ourselves, too, and conquer our internal boundaries.

This book reveals the scene of hidden mental preparation required in the search for the invisible barriers which arise out of one's personality. The book attempts to dig deep into the human mind and pinpoint the regions that ought to be strengthened, just like a muscle.

Players in eSports are interested in honing their skills beyond endless exercises. Personally, my experience so far tells me that exercise and technical preparation can contribute to about half of one's improvement in performance. The other 50 percent depends on the player's mental preparedness and momentary state of mind.

When examining the human mind, even just while considering behavior patterns and the keys to success in eSports, the subject leads to profound recognitions. Thoughts and patterns of behavior on the surface can reveal deeper emotions and motivations. These discoveries in turn may help us be more honest with ourselves and provide a clearer vision about our true goals with an almost childlike clarity and simplicity.

No matter where we come from or who we are, the potential of winning is hidden within us. Beyond the huge amount of physical exercise, we must also get to know our mental processes in order to help us mindfully prepare for the next challenge.

USEFUL **NOTES**

As I planned this book, I made the effort to ensure that the separate subjects follow each other in a logical order. Each of the 10 chapters covers themes that are important to the participants of eSports, addressing topics ranging from physical preparation to inner thoughts and emotions.

Every chapter contains real life stories and lessons that are shown in *italics* in the book. Seeds of wisdom hidden within the lines, that I thought were particularly important, are **highlighted in bold,** the most important ones even **numbered (#)** so they can be reviewed later.

I often wrote many of my own thoughts, and in other pages quoted known thinkers, with the aim to best summarize the gist of a given chapter. In addition, I employed plenty of hand drawings to illustrate the book's many ideas. Because visuals are central to each person's thinking, I tried to stick with the rule that a picture is worth a thousand words.

While putting the book together, I also made sure when introducing a new theme to highlight its application in everyday settings. For lasting development, it is often insufficient to just read a thought-provoking idea; true value is created by testing and applying the concepts in real life, so please be sure to discuss and share them with your teammates and friends.

ESPORTS

eSports require skills of combination and aptitude similar to traditional chess. On the other hand, eSports are different from chess because the players and teams are measured against one another in several types of games.

The games are separated by different categories. There are genres that primarily demand speed and skillfulness (e.g.: Counter-Strike: Global Offensive and Overwatch), or ones that involve planning and strategy (such as Dota 2, League of Legends, and Hearthstone). Players who excel will, naturally, forge these skills during a game and display unexpected moves in their attempts to beat their opponents. Factoring in a certain amount of chance makes these games all the more exciting.

Among eSports, possibly the most interesting are contests where a team of five players on each side faces off in real-time. In these competitions, several variables influence the participants, and each requires the necessary preparation.

Training for eSports is significantly different from training for other sports like basketball. For example, improving physical strength and endurance can greatly influence one's performance on a basketball court. In eSports, however, instead of increasing physical stamina, **technical skills,** **tactics,** and **mental** (psychological) preparedness come to the forefront.

professional basketball player

physical	technical	tactical	mental

preparation time   100%

e-Sports players today

technical	tactical

                                                                               100%

future e-Sports players

physical	technical	tactical	mental

                                                                               100%

Improving our mental state begins while setting our goals, and continues until the last days of conditioning. To comprehensively designate the important cornerstones of an e-Athlete's preparation, it's worth following the model outlined below.

In summary, the stages of preparation can be listed as follows:

1. **Physical preparation**
   a. Physical **conditioning**; rested, relaxed, and balanced states to help concentration
   b. **Technical** preparation; fast reaction time as a result of tons of practice, quick decision-making for unexpected events, confident handling of the platform, heroes, and tools
   c. **Tactical** preparation to learn the game's finer points; mastering the many unwritten rules and combinations of controls that can be quickly utilized at will. These rules and combinations can

be part of a comprehensive individual or team strategy.

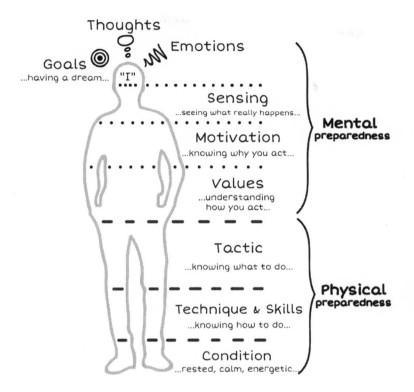

2. **Mental preparation**
   a. Understanding the nature of our **goals**; why we set them and why we want to achieve them
   b. Identifying our merit and assimilating the team's **value**
   c. Recognizing our **motivation**; what drives us during a game and in daily life

d. **Sensing** and attention; how to keep concentration, what causes the loss of attention and how to avoid it

e. Dealing with our **emotions**; recognizing how we often instinctively react to certain situations and how to improve on such reactions

f. Our **thoughts** sometimes wander and, instead of helping, they impede our efforts to achieve the goals we've set

g. **Knowing the self** is essential to living mindfully. Our current state of mind is the total sum of our lifelong experiences, and our ego is just internalized dreams and expectations, often conjured by others. It takes a certain skill to live with self-awareness and to recognize the game our ego plays.

To this day, coaches regard physical exercise (practice) as the key to preparing players, yet we can see from the above list that many of the items relate very little to physical factors. While considering how competitors get ready for an event, we quickly realize that physical workout and strategy are only part of the full spectrum of preparation.

To use an opposite example, imagine being a weightlifter but only pumping iron in your head, learning about building muscles and protein metabolism as a pure theory without ever lifting actual weights. Mental preparation works the same way. No matter how well we know the best strategies or how many times we practice a set of moves, if doubt emerges, emotions can take a hold of us during a game and we won't know how to handle it. The result will be inevitable; physical or mental preparation cannot be swept under the rug, as is often done in the case of the latter.

The average age of athletes in eSports is quite low, estimated between 14 and 26 years old, and this age group can still greatly benefit from sets of mental values, aids, and habits that can be readily acquired. These can also determine one's confidence and successes later in life, even outside of eSports.

If we want to develop a team to ourselves, then we should start to prepare with a complex plan. Exhausting, all-day practices are not sufficient; our mind must be trained as well, with exercises and situations.

The most difficult part of mental preparation is not the discovery of certain key thoughts, but to draw clear conclusions and to build them into our daily life and habits.

1

GOALS AND OBJECTIVE

Our world is a storehouse of opportunities; every day offers new experiences, and it is solely up to the individual to become successful in at their own level, whether in eSports, business, or anything else.

The majority of people live their everyday life without set goals, regardless of the fact that **everybody has hopes and dreams**.

We may recall films in which people live interesting lives where money and knowledge are no object. This often leads us down the path of daydreaming; being a person with unlimited resources, where would we live and travel to, what cool inventions would we realize? Still, relatively few of us convert dreams into actual goals and take the necessary steps to make them a reality.

Without real goals, there is no achievement

The significance of goals is that their appearance brings forth the need for their actualization (1), almost as if they will come to life on their own. Without goals, the need only generates idle daydreaming, which on its own doesn't generate action. Most people accept the fact that dreams do not become a reality, or at least that's what our culture tells us to accept.

A goal is a choice that determines a certain way of life, which leads some to become top e-Athletes, leading scientists, or celebrated chefs – the possibilities are endless.

It's important to **set a goal that is attractive and enduring for us**, so that with time it will remain valid and still be worth fighting for. Fading goals will get replaced, so it's important to choose one that has time-tested relevance. Enduring goals are also solid ones.

As an example, imagine a flag. If the flagpole is not planted deep enough into the ground, the wind will eventually overturn it and the flag will lose its purpose and no longer draw eyes toward it.

WHAT'S A PROPER GOAL?

Anything that comes from the heart. Such is an e-Athlete's desire to excel.

"Let's become the strongest team in the world!"

As soon as we formulate our goal, the questions will follow. What exactly did I mean? On this continent, or on the whole planet? In what capacity? As a competitor or a coach? When we start examining the subject, we realize that there are several ways to achieve a goal. So, we can approach it as something (a) specific or (b) general.

Specific goals are useful because they're tangible and, over time, they take on a concrete shape. General goals, on the other hand, may become less and less clear as time passes.

The solution is to closely link the dream to our goal and paint a detailed picture as the definite objective. This way our goal gains a lifelike quality.

SHORT- AND LONG-TERM GOALS

A short-term goal has a clear plan of action. Short-term goals are like a brief hike where we walk down from a mountain into a valley and the shortest path is clearly visible. Even before taking the route the first time, a map can provide ample guidance to ensure that the trip is easily doable in the allotted time. Short-term goals are very useful for completing a project, but they are best planned if they are part of a bigger objective that we're on our way to accomplishing.

As far as long-term goals, we may not know the path, only the destination. Most of the time at the outset, we don't even know the direction, and we rely only on ideas. During these instances we must start by drawing up a map. To reach the destination, we must rely on our perseverance and determination because we know one thing: it could be a long journey.

What is common with long-term goals is that if we start to seriously describe any of them to a person close to us, the first reaction will be that "we're crazy." This, in fact, is a good indicator that we're on the right path, because the present circumstances are so far from our goal that it sounds insane to attempt to reach it.

"Today I'm an average person with a fresh high school diploma, but my goal is to win with my team in a big city on a faraway land."

The world is full of crazy dreams realized, so it's worth dreaming big.

THE PROPER GOAL IS HONEST AND AFFECTS US

We can't just accept a proper goal, we ourselves must create it. Everybody around us has goals: our parents, friends, and even the organizations that hold the competitions. It's a basic human nature that people want others to work toward their goals. It's in fact an irrational expectation, however, because everybody is too busy to reach all their own goals. To work around this contradiction, people in teams have to align their goals to make them a common one.

We must always be honest with ourselves, and when aiming toward a proper goal, we have to own it. Self-deception only works in the short run while following somebody else's dream, but sooner or later we realize that going down such a path is a waste of time and we want something else.

Many people wish to be rich, but when they encounter a seemingly wealthy person, they heap scorn upon them. If we can't place ourselves, or find it disturbing to be, in a life situation that may be realized through our goal, then we may soon run into an internal conflict that inhibits us from reaching that goal because we're no longer honest with ourselves.

Solid goals strongly resonate even when recalled later. They conjure up images that create positive feelings. When these feelings have a strong effect on us, we know we're on the right track.

THE PROPER GOAL IS WELL ARTICULATED

An important component of a goal is that **it's documented**, so it always stays in focus. This sounds like a minor issue, but many people identify a goal one day and forget it by the next. Then, about a year or so later when they think about that goal again, they confirm with disappointment that it was never reached.

Concerning a goal, the primary importance is not to constantly focus on it and repeat it in our head like some sort of mantra. Yet it has to be strongly rooted in our conscience. For that to happen, it's important to document our goal in a physical form as a first step toward realizing it. If we only think of our goals, their fleeting nature will leave only as much of an impression as a leaf that lands in our hand which also is then quickly carried away by the next gust of wind.

Our goal can be recorded on paper, through a voice recording, or drawn, as children are often fond of. Choose the method that is most personal to you and best mirrors your personality. The important part is to create a permanent record of some sort, regardless of how childish it seems. When it's properly done, it works almost like a time capsule that can only be opened when the goal is reached.

The recorded goal should then be put away for safekeeping. In some schools, such drawings and writings are truly put in a capsule, while others frame them or put them in a secure place.

CONCRETE GOALS WILL REMAIN

The more concrete a goal is, the better it can relate to reality. Many people dream of a home of their own without taking the time to think about its location, size, style, or how to furnish it. Being specific helps to visualize and form a complete picture.

> Goals want to be realized as soon as they're created.

The more detailed is a vision, the more enticing it appears. Cakes, for example, are painstakingly decorated for the same reason.

HOW TO REALIZE A GOAL?

When facing a goal, one of the most difficult questions is how to make it a reality. Everybody likes to daydream, yet most goals remain just that. Many people attribute this failure to lacking the appropriate skills or available resources.

> Reality is more creative than imagination because it doesn't know the term impossible.

Our thoughts are, perhaps, the fastest tools we use because in seconds they can create completely new visions. These are, however, similar to sandcastles on the beach – the first strong wave can sweep them away. **If we wanted to model a real mansion to be built on the beach, sand would be sufficient, but for a real building we'd need professional contractors, appropriate materials, and a solid foundation (2).**

What's unique about our visions is that they can "plant a seed" in our head. That's why some people say to be careful what you wish for.

Goals want to realize themselves

Nature can give us an appropriate lesson for goals realized. Let's take this for example: we want to eat fruits grown from our own tree. How can we make that happen?

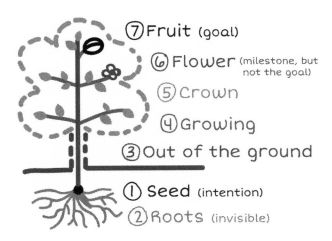

⑦ Fruit (goal)

⑥ Flower (milestone, but not the goal)

⑤ Crown

④ Growing

③ Out of the ground

① Seed (intention)

② Roots (invisible)

1 *First we plant a seed, which is acting toward our goal or articulating our intention. We already know that the better the seed is, the better the expected tree will be.*

The seed in this instance symbolizes our hopes and dreams. We dream about tournaments, great victories, or maybe about fame or happiness. We place our seed with a lot of thought and care in the right place, and we will find our tree there in the future.

2 *Soon the seed sprouts and takes root in the soil. We first won't see anything because it all happens underground, but we water the spot anyway if the dirt becomes too dry or the weather too hot. The roots are our dream taking hold.*

Most dreams need partners to share with, ones who hope for the same outcome. In eSports, they are our teammates. The need for long and solid roots must be emphasized, too, because they will be a key for viability and success when the mature tree encounters several fierce storms in its lifetime. When the individuals spend many hours and days in practice together to build a team, they are also strengthening its foundation.

3 *When the first shoot pokes out of the ground, it's so tiny that it doesn't resemble either a tree nor a fruit. This is, however, the time to take special care, because it's very fragile, easily dries out, and many critters prefer to munch on such young plants.*

Every beginning has a sense of vulnerability, and a starting eSports team also needs plenty of practice before it's ready to compete. A starting team tends to be weak, and if it does not stay in a protective bubble first, it will be exposed to damaging attacks of all kinds from the outside.

4 *Our sapling slowly but steadily grows. It may be a while before it takes a shape that resembles a tree, but more leaves and branches soon appear.*

Patience and perseverance are absolutely essential when nurturing a dream. No magic will make a tree grow faster; it takes as long as it takes. The same can be said about our dreams. Every step takes us closer to its realization even if it sometimes seems that there is no advancing. We may often experience that a project is not moving forward the way we planned it or not taking shape as we designed it. This should never discourage us. We must always remember one thing: **dreams follow our imagination, whereas goals comply with natural forces**. This seeming contradiction, however, is only the effect of a project's self-realization and proof that our tree (or goal) is viable and free to take the best course to grow **(3)**. In the instance of an eSports team, each member will bring their habits and parts of their personalities that will most optimally affect the group as a whole, creating the best dynamic. Nevertheless, every person has their own speed to open up in a group setting. These forces may remain invisible at first and shouldn't even be too heavily influenced so as not to hinder the initial development.

5 *As the branches grow stronger, the leaves form a crown. Our tree becomes more resilient and starts to resemble a fruit tree.*

The team starts to compete in more events and gains more experience against other teams. It survives more encounters but has yet to achieve anything significant. Outside observers notice it – the team suddenly seems to be everywhere. This is the stage where most teams make the mistake of lowering their expectations and giving up their original dream. They reach for a more attainable goal and with that, they obstruct themselves. **Never short change yourself by giving up on your original goal!**

6 *The first flowers appear. Many people give up at this stage, thinking that pretty flowers are not what they wanted.*

In eSports, teams experience certain positive events, when something simply happens. These small, seemingly insignificant happenings – like a direct invitation to a tournament – signify the upcoming change. In a team setting or project development, this is the time to let things happen on their own.

7 *Patience will eventually bear its fruit. After flowering, the tree will return to its original condition, and in a couple of months, small fruits will appear. First only a few of them, but as the tree matures over the course of years, it will produce more than we can take.*

Actualizing a goal goes through the same stages, from planting the seed of intent to reaping the fruits of steadfast labor. The key is goal-oriented persistence.

Persistence is important because our goal won't be fulfilled overnight. If we give up before there is any chance for success, then even all the right steps can't prove their worth because we'll never achieve the result.

Stubborn perseverance will take us toward our goal even if external circumstances get in our way. In a team, we can only control our individual contribution to the common effort, but we cannot win *for* others – only *with* others. To use the example of the fruit tree, thriving **represents the common effort** without which the tree would not grow. During a contest, **thriving to win is the same thing**. When the team competes, what happens individually in each team member's head matters the most while the team acts together toward their goal.

HOW TO WIN THE NEXT MATCH?

In the world of eSports, where advancing happens from contest to contest, the question comes up: what governs the whole process?

Winning the next match can't really be considered a far-reaching goal, and many participants tend to lose their long-term perspective when concentrating on a 30 minute-to-one-hour match-up.

Yet, there is a common criterion between focusing on the next match and the long-term goal. **Neither has its path clearly laid out, and there are plenty of outside variables.** A clearly planned out strategy can help to focus on a proper direction, but it also narrows down the options if the strategy points in a wrong direction. We must remember that **there are many ways to achieve victory**. The objective is not to narrow our options but to widen them. How?

OPENNESS AND WEIGHING OUR OPTIONS

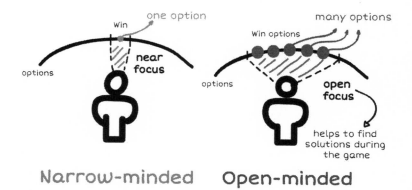

Narrow-minded   Open-minded

Let's keep our options open. If we have several tactics in store when entering the match, then we're better prepared for the unexpected. When we enter a game with such an attitude, we'll be less stressed and more creative.

An open mind is more conducive to creativity, but that doesn't mean that we should charge head-on into our next battle. Creativity usually comes as a result of being in harmony with the game, not by brute force or trial and error.

Often our ego tells us that there is one way toward victory and insists on that way specifically. This sort of view is harmful because **it narrows one's field of vision and takes away many options that would otherwise offer solutions to reaching the goal**. Openness and intuition are very important factors in a contest. By paying attention to small signs, we can plot our course and spot guidance at every turn.

WILL VS. INTENTION

The other important factor in proper preparation for a contest is to not stress about winning, because it confuses the mind by wanting something that has no clear path to being reached. Stress also inhibits creativity.

> If I stress about a goal, I won't remember to find the way to get there.

The right attitude before a contest is to remind ourselves that **we'll give our best to win** so that our minds are focused on that aspiration and will free the necessary inner resources. With this, our mind remains open, and the strategy forms a canvas where our tactic can freely paint the final result.

There is an important difference between will and intention. Will forces a person on a path without a clear vision, whereas intention is similar to a sign-in at a trailhead declaring our plan to get to a certain place. **Intention announces freedom**.

Wanting is akin to dependence, while intention allows letting go. That's why the more tightly we want to hold on to something, the more it slips away between our fingers.

If our goal is to reap the fruits from our tree, then we first have to let that tree free to grow and flower. We will only maim or suffocate our tree by holding onto it too tight.

An intention reflects precisely that sort of letting go; it doesn't nail down the what or the how, but it gives room for creation toward reaching a goal. **When we properly name a goal, we formulate it in a shape of intention, which doesn't strip its power but gives us the freedom to act (4).**

In eSports, making winning a goal works similarly since there are plenty of pitfalls and difficulties between setting off and arriving to victory. There is no universal recipe besides the knowledge that persistence and perseverance leads to winning. Honest and clear intentions influence the team and start the right mental processes even on a subconscious level during the contest. Will, on the other hand, closes the mind with blind focus, creates a false belief that what worked in the past will work again, and oppresses the team members with a "must-win" attitude. Intention leaves room for possibilities and we adapt to the changes while heading toward our goal. When we do the latter, we notice the tiny changes even during fast events, and their hidden information reveals itself to us. If we also notice this on the conscious level, then we know we're on the right path.

LOFTY GOALS

1. Fighting for freedom
2. Helping the needy
3. Fulfilling the dreams of others

What's similar about these goals is that they're **never individually about us**. When people truly serve a higher purpose, their egos fall to the wayside. They don't primarily struggle for personal gain. Nevertheless, fighting for a perceived common good is quite frequent, as it happens while defending a nation or fighting for independence.

Let's use an example in sports.

In 1926, a young boy, named Johnny Sylvester, was lying in a hospital bed with a serious skull infection, when he told his father, "I wish I could see Babe Ruth wallop a homer before I die." The father, who naturally tried anything to help his son's recovery, sent a telegram to the New York Yankees while they were playing in St. Louis. He soon received an airmail package that, among other items, contained a baseball signed by Ruth, who also wrote, "I'll knock a homer for you on Wednesday." Ruth hit three that day.

Both teams, the Cardinals and the Yankees, had an equal chance of winning that day, but while whoever pitched against Ruth, was driven by a personal **fear** of losing the game, The Babe, on the other hand, was propelled by **courage (5)** to help a sick little boy, and most likely fame and fortune that day were far from his mind. (Robert & Thomas, 1990)

Fighting for others, for a goal that points past our ego, always gives an extra boost that no other motivational tool can surpass. Entering a contest in a selfless state of mind makes anybody much more able to concentrate and help to perform with top strength and skill.

AFTER REACHING A GOAL

Even successful entrepreneurs do not measure their level of success only by the money they've made. They know that the key to moving forward after reaching a goal is **to find new paths that take them toward new endeavors**. Whatever we clung to in the past, we must let go of so we can move ahead. The key is to have a variety of experiences. Becoming rich is like getting your favorite food. It can't be the only thing that keeps you going every single day.

Let's open the mind to new things and allow it to linger on subjects that pique our imagination. Children can spend hours with their favorite toys, but they eventually replace them with something new as they grow. Adults aren't any different.

People travel for the same reason: to see different cultures and exotic locations. They want to witness how other people live and define happiness. Many are shocked to find out that in some regions the locals live in relative poverty but still lead a fulfilling and blissful life, thanks to their communal relations or religious devotions.

Life has many flavors, and the only way to experience it is by mustering the courage to get out and take on new adventures.

And the only way to avoid it is by hiding and being stuck in the past.

2

MENTAL SIDE OF **PREPARING**

If we have a goal, we have something to strive for. Yet, constant daydreaming without action has never accomplished anything.

If we want to gain expertise, for example in eSports, then we must start with preparation and practice.

> Becoming a champion is not about talent but hard work.

There are no shortcuts in preparation (6). One step is logically followed by the next in learning and developing a skill. Also, the first baby steps are often coupled with stumbling and sometimes even falling, but that is all natural. This is not the time to be timid, but leaning on an expert can help a lot.

Most of us know e-Athletes who play generally well, but who even after many years didn't become the best among their peers. You may rightly ask yourself, "Why would I succeed?" During practice we must differentiate between (A) deliberate training and (B) pure play. When somebody just plays regularly, even after several years they won't become a professional. This is one of the biggest traps in eSports, too:

until we intentionally target our weaknesses and try to improve on them, we can't talk about focused training with a goal in mind. Many e-Athletes take a long time to consciously decide and start to seriously practice, but they often notice a significant improvement in their skills after only a couple of months that they couldn't have achieved even after several years of playing.

Many individuals are considered "geniuses" or "born to be" something or another. The truth is that the only people who label others like that are the ones who can't see what's behind such a level of professionalism.

The team that keeps winning is not the most talented but the most hard-working.

The best way to illustrate the relationship between an e-Athlete's potential and their performance at an event is by looking at an iceberg.

In eSports we can widen our potentials by improving our understanding of the given game, lowering our reaction time, gaining more experience, and building confidence. These capabilities are only displayed partially during a game, and this can be considered the visible part of an iceberg above the water.

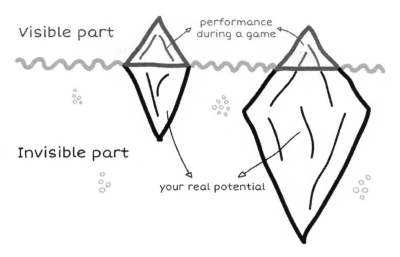

Our real potential is mostly hidden from the viewing audience, but a bigger iceberg has a bigger visible part, too. And that part provides the best show and command of an audience.

To build a deep resource of potential, however, takes a long time and hard work, the subject of which is covered in detail below.

PRACTICE IS A MOTHER OF ALL SKILLS

"It's not that I'm so smart, it's just that I stay with problems longer"
(Albert Einstein)

In eSports the rate of success depends on preparation by 90%. There are no shortcuts when we refer to practice; we either offer full commitment or nothing. With the former, the result will undeniably be seen after a given time. With the latter, or just by giving a half-hearted effort, we only kid ourselves that we're being serious.

Most people don't know it, but synchronized swimming is one of the most difficult modern team sports. The participants usually practice six days a week for eight hours upside down, usually six hours in the pool and two hours on the floor. All this for an Olympic event that lasts for only four minutes each time, requires the team members to perform in perfect coordination, and is undertaken in a partially submerged position that most people would find impossible to repeat. How is it possible to remain underwater in perfect sync with a team? Through an incredible amount of practice, of course.

Hard work always has its reward, but the effectiveness of training depends on four variables.

1. Time spent in practice
2. Number of times each exercise is repeated
3. Quality of exercises
4. Perseverance

TIME SPENT PRACTICING

People in eSports can be categorized by how much time they spend on it.

Most hobby players spend 8-20 hours a week by playing their favorite game, while a professional player could spend up to 60 hours a week, which is a huge difference.

Effective time spent (daily average)	Category
3-4 hours (8-20 hours a week)	**Average** Hobby player
5-6 hours (25-30 hours a week)	**Professional** Full-time player
7-8 hours (40-48 hours a week)	**Determined** Full-time player with outstanding goals
9+ hours (50+ hours a week)	**Fanatic** Full-time player, who dedicates his or her life to eSports

NUMBER OF REPETITIONS

There are many differing opinions regarding the amount of time or number of repetitions necessary for a set of movements or a habit to become instinctive. Based on the research of Philippa Lally et al. (Lally, Van Jaarsveld, Potts, & Wardle, 2010), the observed subjects formed a new habit between 18 and 25 days.

In the instances of fine motor skills, the required repetitions were **100** for it to become second nature to someone. After ✓ that, the given set of movements would confidently work in many different circumstances.

With inadequate practice or interrupted repetition, the set of movements will not get imprinted in the brain. If these required movements are not deployed after a consequent time, there will be no difference as to whether they were practiced previously or not. **Until the moves are repeated at the actual desired times, the level of efficiency with which they are performed will not be reached, either**.

QUALITY AND INTENSITY

The quality of training depends on the level of exercise completed and energy spent in a set amount of time.

For example, suppose we're testing the abilities of a new, unfamiliar character. During these times it's not enough to fill the allotted period with practice, but also to focus on becoming the best acquainted with the character.

Evolution is proof that the key to success is copying. Also, while children develop, they primarily copy their parents and older peers and become quickly proficient in many things, such as walking and talking.

So, let's never be ashamed of learning from others, because that doesn't mean that we become them. The better we're able to reproduce a star e-Athlete's moves and tactics, the more they will become second nature to us and part of our personality. It's like telling a story with our own words. It is based on a source, but shaped by our inner world.

The quality of practice is driven by our own motivation, and after initially learning from others, our degree of perfectionism will determine how good we want to become. We can choose lighter or harder exercises. Nevertheless, top athletes are easy to recognize by how motivated and driven they are just as much during training as while in competition; they always thrive for perfection.

PERSISTENCE

Persistence is an important factor that closely ties to motivation. A great majority of people give up trying something when facing their first major obstacle. In this case, the key to continuing is a sense of persistence.

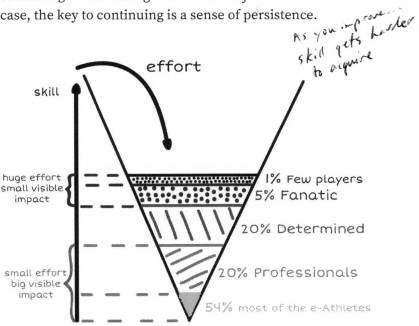

The more a player becomes involved with an eSport, the more they discover its finer points. Initially, success comes easily because at first, the advancement is noticeable. With more experience, however, the invested effort and energy provide only small and incremental improvements because it takes a lot more work and attention to refine and synchronize every single movement, step, and tactic. Naturally, in any given eSport, only a fraction of the participants become top athletes for the same reason: at the

Higher the level more adversity

professional level it takes full-time work to achieve even the smallest refinements, and most players give up prior to reaching that stage.

HOW DO WE IMPROVE?

Among infants it is a well-observed phenomenon that they eat significantly more at weeks 2, 6, 12 and 24. Consequently, the baby's weight jumps during these periods. Among parents, these phenomena are called "growth spurts".

The road to improvement is not linear; it happens in stages.

Many people think that improving skills happens gradually, but in reality it occurs in leaps (7). During continuous practice, new skills sometimes suddenly appear out of nowhere. This happens when disjointed parts finally come together in our heads.

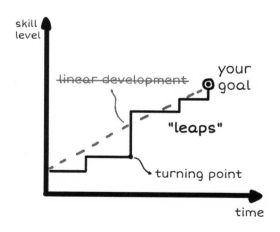

How the brain acquires new knowledge is easily demonstrated by, for example, preparing for a public speaking event. We write down the speech and practice it at length. Even though we start to remember it pretty well, by the end of the day our memory starts slipping. Yet the next morning everything is recalled and suddenly the entire speech comes together. Of course, remembering the content is only the first step, but it's a good place to start before focusing on the next stages, which in this case could be speaking style, volume, posture, and eye contact.

The key to improvement is practice and over-practice. This may sound somewhat negative, but it only refers to the method of reaching beyond an already achieved level. What it does is it forces the brain to reformulate the already-learned patterns and reflect on them from a different angle as the next level tasks come into focus. Using the example of preparing for a speech, when we have already practiced the style of speaking, our memory reworks it without concentrating on the actual words.

Also, for real improvement we must know when to take a break and tune out for a bit. We often feel how after some physical exercise our brain is able to focus a lot better, so proper recreation can help to renew the body and mind. These may be:

1. Reading
2. Exercising, riding a bike
3. Dancing or doing other free movements
4. Meditating, praying
5. Practicing martial arts
6. Making love or doing yoga

Choosing any of the above recreations can help to avoid burnout and maintain internal balance.

RAISE YOUR EXPECTATIONS

STRESSING

Once somebody asked Muhammad Ali, the famous American boxer, how many sit-ups he could do, to which he answered: "I don't count my sit-ups. I only start counting when it begins to hurt, when I can't take it anymore. Well, that's when I start counting..."

Over-practicing for a professional athlete means that during the course of training, the intensity of the exercises should eventually shift from pleasant to tough. Pain is par for the course and it's understood that if the exercise is easy, then the athlete is not working hard enough.

Periodically, we must consciously extend the length of time and the level of difficulty of practices and stick with the plan. Each new level that we achieve that we previously thought unattainable will be a new base to start from. This new base must be reached during every practice session until it becomes easy, and then it's time to aim for a higher target.

The difference between an amateur and professional e-Athlete is the workload, because an amateur player usually doesn't stress about the result. Nevertheless, sometimes an amateur can outshine a professional by approaching a difficult situation with more free and creative thinking. Still, experience counts, and a professional can normally better handle the pressure to compete in the long run.

BREACHING THE LIMIT - OVERREACH

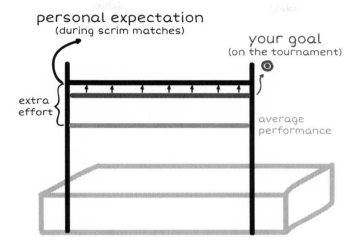

The only way to achieve the impossible during a contest is by proving during training that it's attainable. Overreach refers to the extra effort put into training as the e-Athlete willingly performs above their top performance. Training a game provides a safe environment to attempt such a feat, and it offers a better chance of success while competing.

During such an effort, the coach's role is paramount. Since we all have preconceived ideas about our abilities, we create internal barriers telling us we can't do better that are hard to get over until it's proved otherwise. A coach's task is to create the proper conditions during training so we can attempt the seemingly impossible.

When this happens, we face a new level of stress. Yet, the nature of the human body or mind is that it adapts to even the most hostile circumstances given enough time. And the mind gives up way before the body does, as usually it's the ego that loudly protests and makes its appeals for quitting.

Overreach can't be continuous. By gradually stepping up the level of stress, we're given the chance to get used to the higher demand and move forward to graduate to a higher degree.

For the best e-Athletes, the goal is not just to be the best, but to reach untouchable greatness.

THE IMPORTANCE OF BASICS

Real champions recognize how important it is to build a solid base of skills.

For example, many basketball players reach a professional level with imperfect shooting skills, which causes countless missed points later on. Being too forgiving about basic training is a serious mistake. Top players, for this very reason, consider perfecting their basics not as a chore but a necessity and thorough coaches insist on this even with the best athletes. One may often see champions re-practicing moves and combinations from the previous day's training hours before a game.

Showing pride in perfecting the basics is a clear sign of a motivated player. They understand that perfectly honed basic skills shave off precious tenths of seconds during live events.

Every type of sport, traditional or eSport, holds its secret in the details. To truly know about an eSport, we must delve into its minutiae. The more fine the details we study, the more we can assure ourselves that we're getting advanced knowledge regarding the game. For example, if we have an offensive strategy and want to better our play, there is no better way to study the strategies of defense than to change roles for a few rounds and experience the defensive playing style in our own skin. This is something an average player would never do because "how does offense have anything to do with defense?"

TRULY MASTERING A COMPETENCY

The unique quality of the Chinese bamboo tree is that after the seed is planted, for the first five years nothing happens above ground, even with the most careful cultivation. Then suddenly on the fifth year, in a matter of months the tree can grow as high as 60 feet or 20 meters. For an outside observer, it's an incredible change in a short period of time since the years of hard labor remain invisible. Enduring dreams need strong roots, and the first few years of hard work will spring quick successes in a short time seemingly out of nowhere later on.

According to Noel Burch, it takes four steps of learning to master a new skill (Burch, 1970):

1. **Unconscious dabble** – the e-Athlete doesn't know their level of skill nor the path to knowledge, and even denies that this has any meaning or importance to them.

2. **Conscious dabble** – recognition is gained regarding the value of a skill set and the path to achieve it, but further time is needed to acquire the knowledge.

3. **Conscious expertise** – the e-Athlete can employ their skills but only significant concentration can achieve the same result every time.

4. **Unconscious expertise** – this is the last stage of learning when repeated practice results in reflex-like skills which don't require any significant mental strain. At this stage, the participant can display full competence, and even split their attention to other tasks.

As in many other types of sports, considerable success in eSports is only possible when a player has reached the fourth stage.

TRAIN LIKE YOU'RE COMPETING

As the truism goes:

"As above so below" (Truism)

or its various mutations, such as in music, "there is always a major in a minor and a minor in a major."

Yet many e-Athletes don't take their practices seriously because "it's only practice." The same people usually have a hard time recognizing that there is very little difference between a scrim and a tournament match except their level of tension.

Top e-Athletes who have won tournaments, on the other hand, know precisely that **performance during training has a direct correlation with performance during competition.**

Swimmers also have set cut-off times, so they know the minimum expectation for each event.

Top e-Athletes recognize that during training, they must advance in all facets, be it psychological, physical, or technical preparation.

The more foreign a type of exercise seems, the better it helps to advance.

Bodybuilders know this rule: the weakest parts need the most exercise because they are the best indicators of development.

Coaches spot the most motivated team members ~~while~~ doing the least popular forms of exercise. If a player always gives their best without complaining, then they're on the right path. Such a player usually also excels at crucial moments when winning hangs by a thread during live events.

The same can be said when the team is playing against a weaker opponent. If it performs without motivation, then a stronger adversary may net the same result.

EXPERIENCED VS. NEWBIE TEAMS

Experienced teams always have an advantage over inexperienced ones even if a given day's statistics show otherwise. So, why is that?

The answer is in the accumulation of knowledge.

Let's take the examples of two teams, one with a long tradition of competing and one with a lot of talent but little experience. Both of them reach the finals.

Either of them could encounter a temporary setback with a growing difference in score as the match progresses. The coach of the new team tells them in advance that if they find themselves in such a situation, to stay calm and rely on their skills.

The reason this advice seldom produces a successful outcome is because the players have no prior recollection that they can use as guidance, and facing the unknown causes them to lose faith.

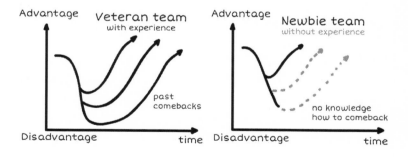

Difference between experienced and newbie teams?

A veteran team can come back from a losing position not only by relying on empty encouragements, but by remembering similar situations from their past and knowing that it's possible to turn things around. Positive memories can be powerful motivators.

Another benefit of having experience is that reoccurring events do not cause any particular anxiety. Fear and a sense of threat limit creative thinking and increase the chance of taking illogical steps. These situations demand the exact opposite; courage and hope leads an experienced team toward victory.

POSITIVE REINFORCEMENT

Positive reinforcement is very important in team communication. It's a form of praise that feeds the ego, gives closure, and fires the team up. The sense of closure helps the players take stock of their accomplishments and the encouragement prepares them for the next challenge.

Praise in eSports is rather rare and few coaches or teammates take advantage of its motivating effect. Yet it's one of the best tools for encouragement.

While delivering positive reinforcement or praise, we should never dilute it with negative comments or expectations. For example, if we say to our teammate that a particular move was very good, we achieve the exact effect we expected to. But if we tell them that the move was good, just next time don't make a mistake with something else, then the praise will produce a negative result **(8)**.

The best analogy is making chocolate milk. Depending on the amount of powder added, the resulting mixture will be more or less sweet. But if we add just a little bit of vinegar to the liquid, we'll spoil the drink, no matter what.

Also, while praising, we shouldn't exaggerate or else it'll lose its validity. A genuine compliment recognizing true achievements can go a long way, whereas flattery may only provide short-term satisfaction.

LET OUR HANDS DO THE WALKING

Once we've devised our game strategy at the beginning of the competition, we should let our instincts take over. Many people believe that this is the point where eSport players must think over every single step, but the truth is the exact opposite. The best move is to calm down and let our muscle memory do the work.

Let's remember, all the training took place so that by the time we got to the event, every move and combination would be second nature. If we try to figure out the right tactics during the game, then we'll focus on many other things besides what's happening.

Our subconscious and muscle memory know exactly the right course of action. We don't have to directly control our hand. Intuitive behavior doesn't enter the conscious mind, so everything happens much faster and more efficiently than if we tried to consider every movement during a game.

effective strategy → several weaker strategies

3

TACTIC AND **STRATEGY**

In eSports, strategy represents a significant role. Correctly selected strategy can be the easiest way to beat an opponent. For this reason, it's common practice now in many eSports to make tactical decisions (choosing the right drafts and tools) prior to a bout. These tactical elements give added advantage during the game.

Choosing an available variation and practicing it during live games can be time-consuming for the team, so it's best to devise strategies in a focused fashion beforehand.

THEORETICAL OR PRACTICAL TEAM

As far as a team's relation to strategies goes, we can identify two opposite extremes. One is where a team perfects a single strategy that it can effectively deploy during its contests. The other is where a team works out as many strategies as it can possibly manage but none to a satisfying degree. While the first team gets seasoned in live matches, the second one experiments with tactics in a controlled environment but has measurable difficulty performing them under real live settings. The first team shows great competence in live events because, thanks to its well-versed tactics, it succeeds against most opponents. If, however, it meets another similar team that deploys an even better strategy, then the team in the first example gets neutralized. The second team has little success, since all the practiced tactics amount to very little without enough live experience. They usually just give up after a while. The optimal solution lies somewhere between these two examples.

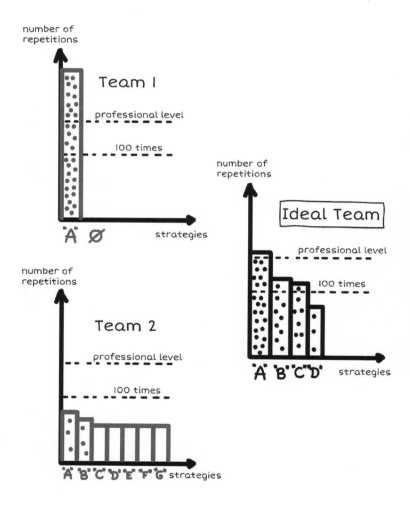

Professional teams are able to effectively deploy several strategies in contests because they invested the necessary time for exercise into every one of them. The key here is the repeated time of practice.

The difference between a simple move and a complex strategy is that the latter is more difficult to ingrain in one's head and requires more repetition.

If you had to perform a single line in a theater piece, it would be quite easy to learn it after few minutes of practice. Strategies in eSports, however, are more like complete stage productions. Actors know exactly how much work it takes to learn and memorize a new theater piece. They go line by line and repeat everything until it's perfect. Association and memorization work best if the words are combined with moves, mimics, and postures, and if the chapters are broken down into blocks following a set timeline. Once the words are learned, it's time to advance on to the next step of practice and focus on the finer points of expressing the personalities of the characters.

STRATEGY BUILDING

Always have a 'Plan C'

Based on the above, the optimal strategies must be relevant to the actual games. We can consider each of them as a "test strategy" because they can only prove their true worth in live trials. After testing them all, strategy "A" is selected, and it's practiced, repeated, and refined to a final form.

Strategies
A /B /C /D /E

70% 20% 5% 4% 1%
usage frequency

A+b know to a fault.

Basically, strategy "A" is favored above all others, and the team chooses it for its effective point-earning qualities. Against unknown or new adversaries, it's the best strategy. Approximately 70% of the time, the given one will suffice, so it's important for the players to know all of its strengths and weaknesses. When the base strategy is selected, it's time to choose a backup strategy that we can call "Plan B." This will be deployed against competitors who are familiar with our posture and prepare against it. Our team will also perfect the "B" strategy and spend the required time to know it in detail.

When memorizing all the strategies, the invested time becomes an important factor. Let's think about it: if we practice a strategy down to its most minute details and perfect it to the point where all the players are finely synchronized, how much time will it take, and is there time to repeat the process for an additional strategy?

TACTIC AND STRATEGY

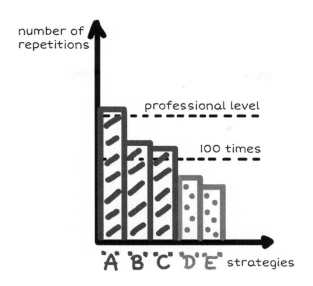

WHEN DO WE NEED A "PLAN C?"

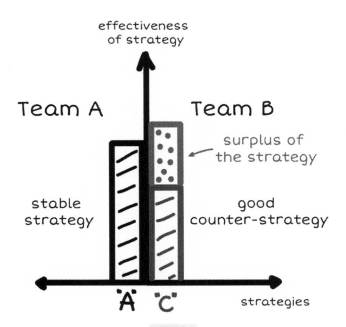

As described earlier, a Plan C will be needed only in rare circumstances, but it needs to be as finely worked out as the main strategy.

There exist many such situations where only a few teams battle it out and each strategy will become quickly apparent (LAN finals).

Another circumstance that may occur is one where we have to overcome a formidable opponent with the element of surprise. It's important that the chosen new strategy will be the ideal antidote to neutralize the opponent's plans. During deployment, the value of this new plan will be found in its unexpected nature. Therefore, it should be well-hidden, hard to predict but practiced enough that it's flawlessly executed.

While choosing the appropriate strategy, we should rely on our first gut feeling. In eSports, the available time prior to matches or rounds is quite short, for example, only about 10 minutes in the case of MOBA (Multiplayer Online Battle Arena) and only 15 seconds in the case of FPS (First Person Shooter) games. This much time is hardly enough to go over a complete strategy and list of possible situations, so relying on intuition comes in handy. Using intuition, however, doesn't equal to banking on random chance. We're not talking about blindly choosing, but rather considering our opponent's options—or at least as much as we can observe— and trusting the wisdom of our intuition when we select a realistic course of action in response.

THE DIFFERENCE BETWEEN STRATEGIES

Main strategies are good if they differentiate from one another by having a distinctly separate stance and by each providing a unique playing experience during a round. It's important not to confuse strategy modifications with strategic alternatives. While in the former, the base—such as the combination of characters—remains unchanged, in the latter the entire basic premise is rewritten. The more clear-cut is the difference between strategies, the more they can be identified as such.

In football, each player learns an average of five-to-six hundred plays from playbooks. When the 11 players take a stand on the field, all of them know their exact positions as the formation is announced. This strategic application in football allows the quick, live application of the most complex offensive or defensive game scenario.

STRATEGY ANALYSIS

Let's think for a minute about the most important strategies we used in the last games. It's possible to examine them from different angles.

1. **Energy requirement**; how physically demanding and exhausting is the given strategy during a round (easy or difficult)
2. **Technical complexity**; how high is the chance for error during the execution of strategy (easy or difficult)
3. **Team play requirement;** in what degree does the strategy rely on synchronization among players or

depend on an individual (team play intensive or individual-focused strategy)

Reviewing the strategies through these metrics helps the team and its coach to determine the best one to choose for a given scenario.

For example, if we're tired, but the mood in the team is high, we can choose a strategy that requires more intensive teamwork but less focus. If we feel fresh but there isn't a true accord in the team, we can select a strategy that demands more focus from the individual. Delivering a good game will raise the team spirit, regardless...

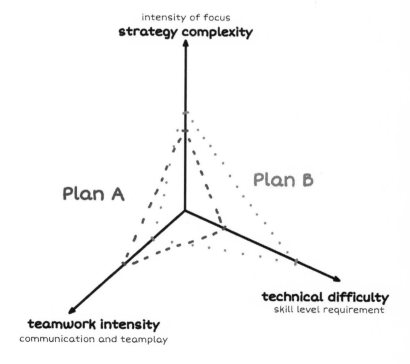

While applying a strategy, we must pay attention to the team members' conditions. **Playing five consecutive games will cause the attention to slack, and that's the best time to use simpler strategies**. It may also happen that one of the players particularly excels in a distinct position, and if it's the right time, we should exploit that opportunity. Many times, players find that they're just right for a role, and they usually perform better when feeling comfortable with certain heroes or situations. It's definitely a tactical advantage that's worth building on and exploiting.

MENTAL STRATEGIES

Most strategic and tactical elements make use of all the available tools and options. The goal of mental strategies is the use of psychological advantage over our opponents when the cards are already on the table.

DRAGON UNDER THE ICE, OR
HOW TO ACT UNPREDICTABLE

As is typical for eSports, the available options are wide ranging.

Let's do something that our adversary least expects. Try selecting a character or arrangement that doesn't fit the pattern of the game, and seems like a confusing choice.

If we force our enemy to stop and think, then they play by our rules. Moving into unknown territory creates doubt and slows the opponent down.

GHOST WITH A MASK, OR
SHOW ONE THING AND DO ANOTHER

We should never show our real intention, but lead the opponent into our trap.

If we play an aggressive game, let's stay calm and defensive on the surface. If we're preparing for an attack, we should conceal our intention and lull the enemy to sleep. Best to hide behind a sleepy-eyed mask.

DANGLING LIVE BAIT, OR
LET'S SHOW OUR WEAKNESS

If we leave an obvious opening, it will allow the enemy to move in for the kill. But by thinking one step ahead of our opponent, behind the opening we can set a trap that they walk right into.

ACTION FOLLOWED BY ACTION

In an average match, it's expected to see numerous deliberate actions, well-versed characters, moves, and combinations from a professional eSports team.

Well-flowing communication reflects the team members' positive mental state, but they become quiet after sudden setbacks.

Children always stay active and are seldom deterred by failure when facing new things.

min.	Team 1		Team 2
1	action		action
	action		
			passive gameplay
10	action		
	action		
			action
20	action		
	action		
30	action		
	action		reaction
40	action		
	action		reaction
50	action		
	action		lost matchup

During a game, the same mentality should be followed whether the play is in upswing or falling apart. The only way to stay present is by initiating action after action. This keeps the communication going even if the situation is hopeless. A game is over only when we give up on it.

In a professional match the number of actions taken is in direct correlation with whether the given team wins or loses. Every active move makes the team hard to predict and puts its opponent off-balance, so even if the initiated action is ultimately unsuccessful, it helps the team keep its first-mover advantage.

PREPARING THROUGH THE OPPONENT'S GAME

"Know your enemy to know yourself."
(Sun Tzu)

Paying attention to the adversary's gaming style and devising a method to neutralize it is almost as important as perfecting our own strategy.

Studying the opposing team is essential before a game, and in eSports there are many opportunities for that through the countless live and recorded matches.

Observing individual players can reveal their thinking and also their weaknesses. This, in turn, should be targeted when playing against them.

On the other hand, the enemy's strengths should be respected and not allowed to be exploited by them. Attempting to directly fight could lead to one's own peril. In battle, sometimes it's unnecessary to counter the opponent's strong points with equal force– even Goliath wasn't beaten by strength but by a well-aimed stone.

STALEMATE OR WRONG DIRECTION?

It's seldom that everything goes to plan, and while deploying a strategy the question often comes up: when does it have to be modified? If things aren't going according to plan then one of two things has occurred:

a. We've reached a stalemate
b. The strategy is leading us in the wrong direction

STALEMATE

Stalemate is like falling off a bicycle. If this happened when we were kids, our wiser elders usually tried to convince us that it was OK and with an encouraging smile urged us to get back on the bike.

Physiologically, stalemate is a condition when the body uses up all its stored sugar and starts breaking down the harder-to-access body fat. Such a stage has the unpleasant symptoms of fatigue, cramps, and loss of mental focus.

Long distance athletes normally try to counter these symptoms by concentrating on an immediate goal. If they fail to do that, their physical fatigue will just stretch out, which is often described as "hitting a wall."

If we reach an impasse during an eSports match, it's the least helpful to concentrate on its reasons. The best attitude is to focus on tighter team play or on the next step in the strategy.

WHEN THE DIRECTION IS WRONG

It may happen that before the game starts the team or captain chooses the wrong strategy to counter the opponent. This shouldn't be confused with an impasse, and the direction should consciously be changed 180 degrees. In this situation, the continuation of the strategy should not be forced, rather the team needs to break out of it and not be lead astray.

There is a chance to make a change during short breaks or even while playing.

During a game it's more difficult to reverse because the players are deep in concentration and filter out any outside noise. Nevertheless, many sports have timeouts, pauses where the team can break the pace and introduce a course correction.

Often just the fact that a timeout is requested signals a need for alteration. When this happens, a quick reminder of what was covered in training brings to life new instructions. Getting a timeout is an essential tool in a game and can literally change the outcome.

During a game, the players themselves could introduce a radical course change, but more often they don't, even while heading toward a certain loss. It's just basic human nature that most of us have a hard time admitting when we're wrong.

Change is uncomfortable and we like to avoid it. By recognizing the need for change, we show courage on its own, so let's not shy away from it.

4

VALUES AND **TEAM**

In 2012 in Ohio State's Division III, girls meet at Jesse Owens Stadium. Meghan Vogel was about to finish her second race of that day. With about 20 meters to go in the 3,200m, Arden McMath, a sophomore from another nearby school, collapsed in front of Vogel. Instead of passing her, Vogel pulled McMath to her feet and carried her across the finish line, making sure that McMath stayed ahead of her.

"Any girl on the track would have done the same for me," *Vogel said later.* (Vogel, 2012)

Real values are hiding under the surface

Values are our ideal aspirations and are linked to our personalities. Their importance is that they are rooted in our core beliefs, regardless of outside circumstances. They serve as guiding principles when we face the unknown.

eSports isn't only about winning, because top e-Athletes recognize that the thrill of victory quickly passes whereas the dream to get there endures.

To be guided by values, let's consider a list of them:

- ☐ Empathy, helping others (be available to others under any circumstances)
- ☐ Thriving for perfection
- ☐ Precision (when every point counts)
- ☐ Commitment, sacrifice to the cause (when we're for something 100%)
- ☐ Self-confidence (not be timid in unknown territories)
- ☐ Honesty (when a mistake is made, accepting responsibility and working to correct it)
- ☐ Open-mindedness (wanting to be more)
- ☐ Problem solver, solution-oriented (not focusing on the problem but seeking a solution)
- ☐ Honesty (truthfulness, straightforwardness)
- ☐ Patience, perseverance 'til the end (we take a deep breath, pause and give time to resist acting out of impulse)
- ☐ Effectiveness (well-devised complex and quick solutions for the given problem)
- ☐ Stability (time-tested, enduring and unshaken)
- ☐ Humility (quieting the ego and recognizing that others' point of views are just as valid as our own)
- ☐ Fight for others, selflessness (paying forward without expecting anything in return)
- ☐ Ingenuity (using creative solutions as the ideal approach)
- ☐ Consistency (committed to a direction; doing as we preach)
- ☐ Courage (going forward where others falter)
- ☐ Sportsmanship (reaching out to shake the opponent's hand even during competition and remembering that we're all athletes)

In a team setting, values are the sum of the positive traits of each member. As they become apparent to others in the team, they thrive to identify with them as well.

It's an exciting experiment to identify a new eSports team's core values and compare them a year later. The result clearly shows the changes that take place individually and communally in a year's passing.

THE SIGNIFICANCE OF VALUES

A team's values become one with the team's name after a while, and the members feel that they are not only represented, but that they also identify with them.

Values become like a knight's armor; the more hardened and better the steel, the more it's worth. Once we put it on, we feel strong and invincible. The team's name and sign are that "armor" that we put on before every game. As children, we could identify with knights because they had noble goals in our favorite stories. They believed in the kingdom, justice, and that the righteous will vanquish the forces of evil. If the team represents the individuals' values, then the members proudly wear its emblems and feel true cohesion.

Every type of eSport manifests itself through the athletes. The story they create is written on the field of competition. Storytellers and e-Athletes thrive for the same thing, to create a perfect story that is their own. What's more important than the story, perhaps, is **why** it's told in the first place.

For an e-Athlete, values provide a solid base of commitment. Some pursue eSports to make their parents proud. Some do it for the sense of belonging and self-realization in an eSport community. When these values are common in the group, they become the team's values.

TEAM SPIRIT AND CULTURE

Team spirit is based on the group and its common goal. Even though the members will never agree on every single thing and will remain as individuals, the common goal will make them fit together like gears and cogs in finely-tuned machinery.

So long as the members of a team don't recognize that their strength comes from their common accord and not from their individual talents, they won't be able to perform to their best potential.

Every team has a weakness but can turn it to its benefit by finding a playing style that mitigates that weakness with a common approach.

Many people struggle with the idea of team spirit. It becomes most apparent before a game when the team is getting ready. How do we know if there is true synergy within the team? When common habits, inside jokes and signs, or the tolerance toward the others' personal traits are noticeable.

Team spirit gives an extra boost for a better game and better communication, which helps us excel above other teams.

WE ARE ROWING TOGETHER

The most important thing for leaders and team members is to optimally manage their roles in the team.

To best demonstrate this we can look at the assigned functions in a row boat.

The coxswain (coach or captain) steers and leads (the analogous team member in most eSports even rows). Their role is to make the team follow a strategy while piloting the boat. The rowers (players) use their full strength to propel the boat toward the finish line and make every effort to perfect and synchronize their rowing motion. Of course there are also refined roles within the team that come from each member's personality.

What are the problems that could come up regarding our rowboat?

1. The *coxswain* is not piloting the boat correctly – the right direction is essential if the team wants to succeed.
2. A *rower* is not pulling their weight – this becomes apparent quite soon to the rest of the team and

everybody starts slacking during practice and competition

3. A *rower* is using the wrong rowing technique – this slows the whole team down

4. The *rowers* are not in sync – during strategizing the team plans out at what stage they will use how much strength during the row. If there is a lack of communication, the boat's speed is not going to change much.

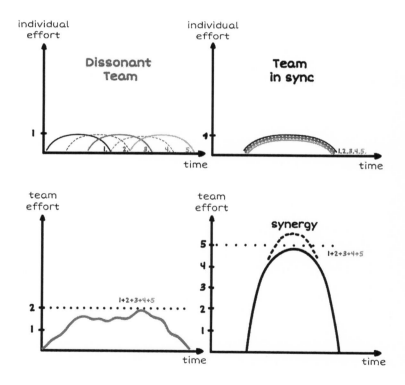

What's unique in rowing sports is that one member can completely negate the entire team's effort. In eSports this translates as noise in team communication. Slight miscommunication time-to-time is inevitable in any team, but if it's not promptly corrected, the team will never reach its full potential.

In a team's lifespan, synergy—the phenomenon where the total effect is greater than the sum of individual effects—is an important factor. If there is unity and the performances add up, the potential opens up for creative solutions that outside spectators may consider impossible.

HUMILITY

A person shows humility if they're able to (1) pay attention to others during conversations and participate in the even exchange of information, (2) keep their ego in check, and (3) hold a mirror up to themselves to learn from mistakes and be honest.

Humility is not an attribute but a key to development.

The challenge is to be big while staying small. Humility is not a human trait but a condition. Many people mix up humility with being subservient. Yet the two aren't the same.

Humility is being able to see past our ego. If we work in a restaurant and the only thing that occupies our mind is how much more our friends earn or how miserable we feel, then we rob ourselves the experience of the joy we bring to our guests with a plate of great food and good service.

For an e-Athlete, humility reflects the intent to develop. The e-Athlete who wishes to be better catches the attention of the coach by **listening to and following instructions**. They also unceasingly observe their opponents to learn from them. They pay attention to optimizing even their smallest movements. They formulate insightful questions to gain valuable knowledge from the answers **(9)**.

Observing others, however, doesn't mean slavish copying, but the exact opposite. Seeing and hearing everything provides a chance to test out observations and to see what works.

Others can't provide us with turnkey ideas (not even coaches can do that) and we can't expect to learn something without doing it. To make an idea our own, it must be applied in practice. The same happens through the outright rejection of an idea; if it's not tested out, we won't know for sure whether it's useless or not. This is why teachers know for certain that students **who agree or disagree with everything will learn nothing**.

MODESTY TOWARD OURSELVES AND OTHERS

Being humble—as opposed to feigning modesty to stroke our ego and receive praise—is important in an athlete's development. It shows that they haven't reached their desired goal yet. After reaching a major milestone or getting positive feedback, it's good to get the right perspective. If not, a partial victory leads the ego to believe that it is a final one.

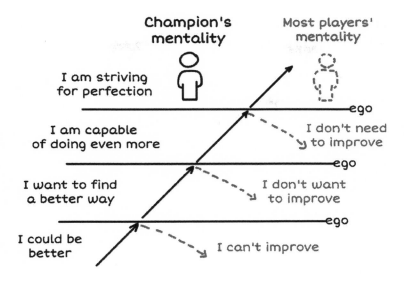

Champion's mentality

Most players' mentality

I am striving for perfection

I am capable of doing even more — I don't need to improve

I want to find a better way — I don't want to improve

I could be better — I can't improve

ego

ego

ego

The only boundaries for you are those you place in front of yourself

On the other hand, if we're honest with ourselves, we recognize that partial achievements are only markers toward our final goal.

True champions do not consider obstacles as such. They see endless possibilities, limitless improvements, and boundless advancements. True champions enjoy their sports, consider every victory as merely a stopover to the next one, and are motivated by the journey in their careers.

RESPECTING THE OPPONENT

Most teams view their opponents as their adversaries since they consider the games as battles. Yet the truth is our opponents are quite like us. They have the same sort of dreams and fears. The funny thing is that they're more similar to us than our very own friends.

Many e-Athletes consider the other team as people in the military view their enemies on the battlefield. But we can observe that a true sportsmanlike attitude dictates that once the game is over, the opposing players congratulate each other for the good fight. The beauty of eSports is that they're like board games, and everybody wins once in a while.

LEARNING FROM THE OPPONENT

When we're beginners, we enjoy watching the professionals play and dream about becoming just as good. Even if not consciously, we store a lot of the information we witness regarding different moves and strategies.

This interest, however, slackens once a player reaches top ranking because often the ego tells the e-Athlete that they only have to perfect their own style. In eSports, as in many other sports where the games can be recorded and replayed, reviewing previous matches helps to define many aspects of style, tactic, and strategy for later improvement. But why not let the best players be our masters? In eSports, people playing in the same role as us provide a unique point of view that we can observe and analyze to learn its differences. The key is not to copy what others do, but to gain a fresh perspective and consciously consider other approaches for future rounds.

Learning from our opponents is one of the best ways to improve (10).

EVERYBODY'S EQUAL

In reality, nobody is better or worse than others, only different in some ways. Some may call this an idealistic view because our moral, social, and economic codes rank us in a very real way. Yet, being rich, disabled, young, fat, or criminal are all relative and only labeling the individuals makes them so. The truth is, we come to life as new beings with nothing and leave this world with nothing, at least in terms of material possessions. Anything that happens between these two states is in many ways our own doing, our own experience, and our own labels that we accept and wear.

Recognizing that we're all equal is important because people like to measure themselves against others, even though the difference is an illusion. Our ego likes to play this game because that noisy and judgmental part of our identity only exists in relation to labels and though comparison with external things. It feels so real that we let it most of the time pronounce the final say on why we fail and how we should be judged based on outside factors.

FLAMING OR BLAMING OTHERS

Flaming has become an art form in today's world. Flaming is generally when we express ourselves through blaming others. When we do this, we try to divert attention from our own failings and attempt to appear in a better light. We feel that it's necessary to do that because admitting a mistake opens us up to outside criticism. Unfortunately, this damned-if-you-do-damned-if-you-don't situation is indicative of our "blameless" society.

When somebody is found at fault, they suddenly become exposed to the risk of being shunned by their peers or excluded from a group. The ego, which is hypersensitive to social ranking, tries to protect the individual by shifting the blame to other persons or outside factors.

Blaming, however, isn't solution-oriented, because discovering a mistake does not equal finding a remedy. Blaming an unplugged toaster for not working won't fix it, but plugging it into an outlet will.

In teamwork, real solutions happen the same way. Emotions won't advance the group and, at best, our ego will be the only one satisfied by diverting blame.

LASSIE AND LOYALTY

Most of us know Eric Knight's fictional character, the trusty canine heroine Lassie. The story focuses on one of the dog's main traits – loyalty. There is a true-life parallel that is similar to Lassie's story, about an Akita named Hachikō, who was a Japanese professor's dog in the 1920s. The two of them lived in the suburbs of Tokyo. Hachikō always came to the train station to greet his master when he returned from the university in the evenings. The two continued their daily routine, until one day the dog's owner failed to come back because he had suffered a fatal brain hemorrhage during the day. Although the professor's gardener took in and cared for Hachikō after his owner's death, the loyal dog steadfastly returned to the station at the same time every evening for the next nine years, all the way until his own passing.

Animals' ingrained sense of loyalty is present in all of us humans, too, and it's deeply embedded in our instincts. The only thing that inhibits us from allowing this feeling to take hold in our relations to others is our egos. Often this is even present in family environments; although due to the closeness and the amount of time spent together, family members have better opportunities to work out their differences. Nevertheless, the game of push-and-pull to a certain degree remains present even in decades-long relationships.

Members of a team relate to one other in a similar way to family members: initially they learn about each other's most apparent habits, and later about their hidden sides. But the more time they spend together, the closer they get, and loyalty toward their mates becomes increasingly fierce with each passing match.

5

MOTIVATION

When we talk to an eSports tournament participant after winning a game, we realize how much motivation they had during the match. We see what was behind the amount of energy and persistence that was displayed.

A motivated e-Athlete's ability to perform is many times over that which an average person is capable of. But the increased level of performance and focus also brings along the requirement for much longer and more complex practice sessions.

How far can we get?

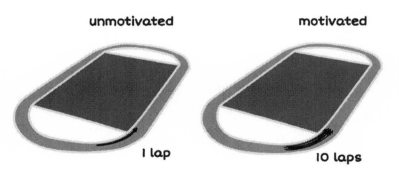

unmotivated   motivated

1 lap   10 laps

Often the motivation that drives an e-Athlete is not at all obvious, so next we'll attempt to investigate its nature and how it functions.

WHERE IS MOTIVATION COMING FROM?

Motivation toward performance is shaped in childhood. Children form their behavior by copying their parents, even for things like diligence, hurrying, and perseverance. For this reason, if a parent wants to instill positive attributes in their child, the best way to do it is by **being a positive example**. No matter how much we urge our children to not give up or to study hard, if they experience the exact opposite from us they will not achieve it. Children see and sense exactly how persistent or patient we are.

I was around ten when I saw my mom preparing her term papers. She moved into seclusion, often for several days at a time, making short-hand notes as thick as a book. Of course, she passed her exams with flying colors. But what stayed with me was seeing the determination and energy on her face, completely immersed in her work, as this small boy walked around her utterly unnoticed. Since that time, I've put the same demand on myself that I've seen from my mom.

MEMORIES OF CHILDHOOD

If we want to know our deepest selves, then we have to discover our own pasts. Many people don't realize how much they can resolve in their present-day problems by looking for answers in their childhood.

For me, sports always had a special meaning because I was very competitive. I loved to play soccer. I knew I wasn't as skilled or talented as some of my peers, so I started studying the best players and copied their moves until I could do them myselft, run as fast and kick as well as they could. Then I could play with them as equals.

Today I do the same: I learn from the best and practice until I am capable of doing it a more perfect way, which, in my view, is good enough.

What happens to us as children provides the answer to our present attractions and needs. Motivations are especially interesting because they're sometimes rooted so deeply in our conscience that we don't even know the true reason for their presence.

RECALL

People can remember more of their childhood experiences than they assume. The key is to let the memories come up on their own.

For example, do we want to know where our passion for a certain thing comes from? We simply must ask the right questions.

"Why do I love coffee?"; "How did I get so competitive?"

Let's allow our memories to come to the surface that perhaps don't even tie directly to the inquiry, but let's relive the related situations. If we do this right, the key moments will suddenly reappear, and they will shed some light on how the habit formed, on what was the original motivator.

This technique helps us to know ourselves better, to redefine our actions, and to aid us in making more conscious decisions. The key is to ask the right questions.

THE INTERNAL FACTOR OF MOTIVATION

The internal factor of motivation is passion: the drive to learn something new or to shift an ability into another dimension.

wood we add
(sense of success)

flame
(strength of motivation)

starter
(parental model)

Motivation is like a campfire. Behavior patterns learned from our parents are the kindling. In our teenage years, the sparks that we feel for eSports or for gaming ignite the fire. Two components keep the flames going: (1) the starter, which is the perseverance learned from our parents, and (2) the wood that we add to the fire – our sense of success. Many people never become top players in eSports because they do not experience the joy of accomplishment. Others become top athletes by getting a sense of positive reinforcement and truly open their wings.

We can distinguish two groups of top players. The first group identify themselves by positive feedbacks, compliments and rewards they get. They're motivated by the recognition they receive after winning an event. Individuals belonging to the other group view winning as a form of self-realization, and they're recognized for their unyielding perfectionism. These people always have a hidden store of self-motivation that helps them go the "extra mile" during the practice. They are the ones who become champions in eSports.

FACTORS OF MOTIVATING PEOPLE

Every person has basic needs in their life. According to the model conceived by the American psychologist Henry Alexander Murray (Murray, 1938), many of these needs have different levels of importance for each individual. The most important and common ones are certainly present in the lives of e-Athletes as well.

☐ Vital needs – nourishment and breathing are aimed at self-preservation

☐ Need for attention and performing to others – people are social beings, so others' attention is essential for normal communal interaction

☐ Need to adapt – finding one's place in a community, following signs, symbols, brands, and styles

☐ Security – looking for support, finding anchors in life

☐ Yearning for a partner – establishing a relationship based on mutually shared emotions

☐ Independence – standing on one's own feet

☐ Need to influence – preferring to influence others and enjoying the role of being influential

☐ Being successful – our self-confidence grows when we receive feedback that our daily passion is beneficial

☐ Paying attention to ourselves – other than enjoying the attention of others, taking care of ourselves is important. Yet it can manifest in an overly positive or negative fashion, such as self-love or self-pity.
☐ Oral gratification – alcohol, tobacco, gastronomy
☐ Sexual urges – extremely strong natural need that can even go against social conventions
☐ Gaming needs – people favor imaginary situations and games where they can satisfy their urges that would otherwise be left unfulfilled in real life; a common theme in all eSports.
☐ Curiosity – a need to examine, being drawn to the unknown that is natural in most humans

Motivation is closely connected to needs, as it is powered by them. For example, if somebody gives importance to oral satisfaction, that person can be easily motivated by the promise of a nice dinner.

So, in essence, motivational factors are framed by satisfying needs and symbolizing their fulfillment.

Related to eSports, the following important factors can be identified:

1. (External) Caring and attention – my team accepts me; the fans follow my achievements
2. (External) Feedbacks – compliments and recognition; influential people recognize my values
3. (External) Money and reward – prizes and payouts won at eSports
4. (External) Fear and condemnation – fear of the coach's wrath or of getting removed from the team

5. (Internal) Success and joy – enjoying the game and having success
6. (Internal) Thriving for perfection – self-fulfillment in eSports

The listed factors hold varying sway over the e-Athletes depending on which ones are the strongest in each of them. Some are motivated by success alone, others yearn for recognition from their fans or parents, yet others want nothing more than to receive financial rewards.

As far as motivation, the only thing important is to recognize our own needs and to know what is truly significant.

WHAT IS AFFECTED BY MOTIVATION?

Motivation basically works in two ways. It can affect **persistence** or **quality**.

MOTIVATING PERSISTENCE

Persistence has a time factor. For example, e-Athletes can be given incentive by rewarding extra training and spending extra time to practice certain moves. The same result can also be achieved under threat and by inducing fear as a subconscious motivation. Fear and reward are considered **external motivators**.

MOTIVATING QUALITY

Motivation that affects quality normally originates from inside, so it is considered **internal motivation**. Internally motivated e-Athletes may spend an extra hour practicing not to satisfy somebody else with the added time of training, but to truly hone their own skills.

Some basketball players arrive to practice hours before the training begins so they can work on some basic skills, or stay after to really refine certain moves. In this case, quality doesn't only appear through extra time but shows the player's care and attention to make the most of the available span of time.

Self-motivated athletes are easy to spot because they work the hardest during the entire practice session and exert all their energy by pushing their limits.

Internal motivation should be valued in everybody because it's the sign of genuine enthusiasm for a certain thing.

THE CANDLE PROBLEM

Sam Glucksberg, a professor at the department of psychology in Princeton, tested the "candle problem" on individuals (Glucksberg, 1962). The experiment had originally been invented by the Gestalt psychologist Karl Duncker in 1940s.

The items in the candle problem were a table next a cork board wall, a small tray of thumbtacks, a candle, and a box of matches to light it. The experiment called on the participants to fasten the candle to the wall so the wax doesn't drip on the table.

The group of individuals were told that their performances would give guidance on how fast on average other people will typically be able to solve the problem in later experiments (internal motivation).

Candle Problem

A second group was told that if they were among the fastest in solving the problem, then they would receive a substantial monetary reward (external motivation).

To solve the problem, some amount of creative thinking must be performed, because the tray that holds the tacks is also needed. By fastening the tray to the cork board with the tacks and standing the candle in it, the task is properly accomplished.

Interestingly, the experiment produced the odd result that the group of individuals who were given the external motivations was less successful in solving the problem than the others.

Behavioral researchers attributed this result to the fact that performing to earn tangible rewards creates stress, which forces the individual to increase their focus. This, in turn, lowers the brain's capacity to think creatively. Members of the other group, who were allowed free rein without external pressure, had better luck with creative thinking, and the reward came internally in the form of succeeding to solve the problem.

The same can be said about the prevailing conditions in eSports competitions: focus and stress may get a player from point A to point B successfully, but generally creativity advances the player further. And for this, having an **open mind** is necessary, which is produced by the driving force of internal motivation.

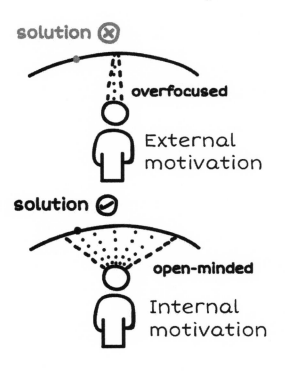

Finding the solution during difficult matches is done not by insisting on deliverance of well-practiced strategies, but by **opening our minds to all possibilities (11).**

OUR HEROES

We learn from the ones who we like, those close to us, those who stir our emotions and whom we look up to. We use people as examples, the ones who deliberately or unconsciously pop into our heads when we recall things that we learned in the past. They're our everyday heroes.

For coaches and captains, who are leading teams, it takes time to build such a reputation. No matter how much they and their leading styles are liked or hated at first, the important thing is to create an emotional connection with their teams. But the surest sign of ineffective leadership is an indifferent team.

The unique thing about setting an example is that people tend to follow them whether they love them or hate them. This is especially noticeable in parent-children relationships where the children clearly repeat their parents' patterns of behavior without differentiation.

ELEVATE OUR PLAY STYLE TO AN ART FORM

Many e-Athletes, when asked what motivates them, reply that they try to achieve perfection. This attitude is basic to human nature and it's most clearly apparent in artisans of all kinds who spend huge amounts of time refining the smallest details of their handiworks. They typically emphasize the uniqueness of their creations and the attention that was invested into making them. This attitude is true for painters, musicians, craftsmen, and athletes of all kinds. We can witness a perfect form or action in eSports that gives nearly as much pleasure to the player as winning the match.

In eSports, the game is the raw material, the character is the tool, and the match is the final creation. Loving the game is very important because that generates the joy when playing it to perfection.

MOTIVATIONAL SPEECH

Motivating a team by standing up and speaking in front of them is an important arrow in a coach's or leader's quiver. Interpersonal communication remains one of the most effective ways of passing information. Motivational speech, however, is different in its style and substance than simply speaking to others.

The information conveyed in a motivational speech is always quite basic, and it can take the form of **giving thanks** or **emphasizing value** and **honesty**. It can also reinforce a belief in the team's **ability to win** or in the idea that it's not all about winning. The leader can also boost the team by **reassuring that they will stand behind them 100%, no matter what**. The purpose of a motivational speech is to give the needed extra emotional support when the strategy and tactics are already perfected but the team lacks the spirit to reach its goal.

Motivational speech is not a deception to connive extra performance, but is an expression of honest feelings shared with the team to reinforce the bond between them and the speaker, and a means of giving courage to a team.

6

THE **SELF**

THE ATTENTION

Our inner self is best described by understanding how attention works.

Attention works by staying quiet and making a connection. When we look at another person, we begin to build an invisible bridge. Often when we watch somebody in a crowd, they notice it and turn around even if they had their back to us. Some people claim that attention carries its own charge.

Attention is stronger between two people when there is eye contact. As eyes are called the mirror of the soul, a mental bridge finds its connections when the people communicating lock their gazes.

Attention works differently in other situations; for example, when actors are on stage and draw the eyes and ears of several hundred people, they get an immense amount of energy from the spectators. The same thing happens in a college auditorium, where students are listening to a professor's lecture. Yet this type of engagement is asymmetric, because the information flow is one-directional.

A similar situation can also occur in interpersonal communication if one person dominates the conversation so much that the other is reduced mostly to the role of a passive listener. When this happens, the silent party of this one-sided discussion is usually left drained, while the other, unknowing of what has just transpired, may describe the conversation as fun and engaging.

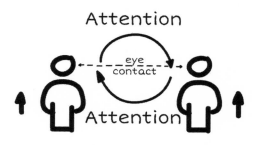

Flow of attention

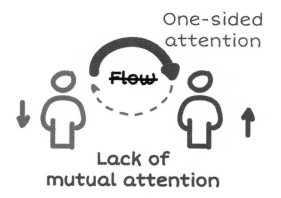

**Lack of
mutual attention**

GETTING ATTENTION

People first learn to communicate as babies by trying to get their parents' attention. It happens primarily at the most basic levels: crying, smiling, and making rudimentary sounds, but effectiveness is quickly learned by registering the **rewarding experience (attention)** that follows such attempts **(12)**.

As adults, we constantly hone our skills of getting attention because of its learned social benefits.

THE GAMES

The purpose of playing games, similar to a theatrical performance, is to get someone's attention and be charged by it. The types of games some people play are distinctly different from one other. Some are spectacular, others are odd, but their purpose is almost always to get a reaction – either positive or negative – from the person who is the target.

Eric Berne, in his book Games People Play (Berne, 1967), called this phenomena "human gaming."

The most common types of games are tied to personality traits and these traits are as follows:

1 **Menacing** ("the very air freezes around them") – Menacing game is exemplified in the person who tries to dominate by instilling fear in others.

2 **Blabber-mouth** ("they can't keep quiet") – There are people who keep others occupied by endless chatter. They typically have difficulty following other people's trains of thought, and if somebody else is finished talking they just continue with their monologue.

3 **Provocateur** ("Where did this come from") – There are people who like to shock others with outrageous embellishments, strange behaviors, or strange outfits. They try to be different at any cost.

4 **Porcelain doll** ("they act like a princess") – The porcelain dolls use their beauty and refined styles to draw attention to themselves, but don't feel the need to be an extrovert. They often stay emotionally distant from their surroundings and remain cool or unapproachable.

5 **Adventurer** ("they care about sports not people") – The adventurers are often introverts, but with specific goals that sometimes seem intense to an average person. Many of them are pure adrenaline junkies and pursue sports that are extreme in nature. For them, friendship is secondary to their passion, but they like to talk about their adventures and enjoy the attention in a group.

6 **Inquisitor** ("they dig into others") – A conversation with an inquisitor always feels like being examined. They interrogate until they find a personal and sensitive subject, which they deconstruct down to its smallest details. Such discussion is quite intense, torturous, and overpowering for the other person.

7 **Poor me** ("they feel sorry for themselves") – This sort of person loves to complain and always finds a reason to earn the pity of others. The poor-me person gains emotionally if they receive comfort.

8 **Secretive** ("they're a mystery") – These introverts don't share much about themselves and don't talk much either. On the rare occasion when they speak, they try to sound as thoughtful as possible to reveal their intelligence and pique the interest of others.

How one gets other people's attention determines the personality of an e-Athlete. There are people who constantly crave compliments, feedback, or encouragement if mistakes are made. While still others play a whole season silently; these players consider the few occasions to be more significant when the coach pats their back and gives a compliment. There are others who only play for the crowd and measure their successes by the number of fans they acquire. And some consider their team a family and are motivated by their encouragement.

One thing is common: everybody needs attention and recognition in a team.

QUEEN SYNDROME

To better understand the effect of attention in a star e-Athlete's life, let's examine a certain type of personality that we will call a "queen" as an example.

The queen is a young woman with radiating beauty, an irresistible smile, and a captivating personality. Even when she was a young princess, everybody noticed her ideal features, and she was regularly fawned over. As she grew, the attention she gathered increased. Soon even the boys fought over her and tried everything to earn the right to be in her company.

So what's behind all this? Because of her beauty and status, this young girl gets tons of attention, which feeds her ego.

People around her watch her every word. She, on the other hand, doesn't have to pay attention to anybody because she enjoys a steady supply of fans regardless. This eventually results in her lack of ability to be reciprocal while exchanging information with her peers.

As time passes, her ego becomes so insatiable that it demands the attention of ever more famous and influential people. She realizes that displaying her wealth and splendor can get her into the finest circles of individuals. Her ego by now is so skewed that she can't approach anybody without prejudice and she views all human contact through the filter of her expectations.

SUCCESS AND INCREASED ATTENTION

The above example is essentially unique, but there are individuals who have to do very little for success because they can conquer their world with good looks alone. Still, anybody can be successful in something.

Many children start to pursue a type of sport at a very young age precisely because they see how popular are its top athletes, how often they can barely move while surrounded by adoring fans.

This type of attention is what the previous "queen" has enjoyed. The athlete suddenly notices that a successful career is closely followed by growing circles of people who are no longer related to coaches and teammates; they're personal assistants, managers, and thousands of fans. The amateur becomes a professional, as they say. Yet the success didn't fall from the sky; it was the result of long and hard work.

The athlete's life radically changes and at once the traits of the young queen begin to appear on them. Hiding from the public becomes a norm, staying in direct contact with only the people who serve their daily needs.

In this instance, though, the personality of the athlete enjoys a great advantage over the young queen's, because starting out as equals teaches another perspective. This initial experience trains the ego to remain steady unless it experienced no attention whatsoever during childhood. In that case, success can be outright detrimental.

Successful people have some difficulty protecting their egos from the intoxicating feeling of attention, which can be quite addictive. But if an e-Athlete gets controlled by this feeling, they can easily be led astray and lose the essential focus to carry on.

THE SELF WE KNOW

If we look into ourselves, we can recognize that our dreams are like a double-edged sword. We enjoy being at the center of attention, but at the same time feel bad if somebody we care about is being ignored in the same setting. At times we're at peace with ourselves, and other times we struggle with internal conflicts; we can be our own worst enemies, and we can achieve unbelievable feats.

In order to understand this duality, we must examine the effect of environment on the person. Let's think of newborns; they're, as they say, pure and innocent, unpolluted by the coarseness of the world. But as they grow by the side of their parents, little by little they learn that mom can be sad and dad can be stressed, and they **pick up on the ambience of their immediate surroundings**.

Children quickly learn that certain patterns of behavior can manipulate their environments. If they cry, they promptly get proper attention, and if they do something to gain a reward, they will most likely get it. Experience teaches them that the environment can be changed, but there are also unexpected things beyond their control. They cannot at first conceptualize why people hurt one other and they, in fact, remain unaware of their own jealousy.

Competing becomes an everyday habit and by the time they enter school, they know that certain behavior, even if it's negative, earns more attention and is better rewarded by the teachers and other parents. These learned patterns don't come naturally but are conditioned in children as they witness the results of their behavior in the world around them.

Ego (Outer self)	Inner self
Me	We
Egoist	Altruistic
Conservative, prejudiced	Creative, open-minded
Focuses on the external world	Experiences the world as whole
Past or future oriented	Now-oriented
Pursues pleasures	Self-realization
Will	Intention
Struggles	"Flows"
Measures	Accepts
Recharges from others' attention	Recharges by experiencing
Expects	Offers
Possesses	Lets go

As the childlike innocence is slowly buried under social conditioning, the young individual learns how to adapt to group behavior – not to stand out and be ostracized. Most people, by the time of reaching their thirties, have perfectly adopted the society's norms and demands, and completely forget their childhood dreams, the things that made them so happy. **This newly-formed shell or external self is the ego. The instinctual childlike wisdom in the core of a conscious being is the inner self.**

The table above lists the differences between how the self expresses itself on two separate levels. Notice how each layer of consciousness relates and acts.

Still, why separate the two sides of what we consider our self-identity? So that we can recognize the difference between our core being and the layers that have accumulated on it over the years, which can be changed.

EGO

The majority of people enjoy going on vacation and can barely wait for this couple of weeks of rest, to be undisturbed and to do as they please. When the holidays come, they usually go to their special places in the mountains or spend time by a body of water somewhere. Yet, while vacationing, their usual problems pop up again. It's too hot, they're too tired, the wait is too long, or they're too stressed right before dinner. The truth is that when people go places, they assume they can feel different without consciously trying to be different. And of course, we can change our surroundings but that won't change who we are.

Everybody has an outer self that's shaped in large part by social conditioning and that comes to being while first interacting with parents and other caretakers. The ego's role is the constant search for self-gratification and self-preservation, sometimes even at the expense of others. Nevertheless, the ego isn't evil, just as a predator isn't for killing other animals.

In many Eastern religions, the ego is consciously kept in check, and by holy practitioners it's reduced to an absolute minimum. Yet for westerners this equates to overkill. **The solution for us is keeping our egos in harmony with our true selves by making conscious choices.** The ego only becomes overpowering if it's allowed to be the sole decision maker.

We can best understand our egos by identifying how our actions are dominated by certain patterns of behavior. For example, when we struggle to make a decision during a match, it's the ego that's taking charge at that moment.

By its definition, it may appear that the ego is something negative, but its failings are not because of its attempts to explain the outside world and react to it. The weakness of ego originates from its slavish repetition of negative patterns of behavior and its greed for getting attention.

THE INNER SELF

Many of us realize during our lifetime that we only live to please others, not to find a true purpose or fulfill our destiny. When this happens, that sudden realization tells us that we always do as we're told, while our desires are slowly forgotten and wither away.

If we wake up one morning and realize that we no longer know our wishes and cannot recognize ourselves, then it's time to change.

Change is only attainable by breaking the connection that forces us into dependence and by beginning to focus on ourselves. We must spend time alone and be occupied without others being around. The answer to life's big questions and our greatest desires are hidden within us; they just need some time to reveal themselves.

When we were children, pure and simple, we could readily and honestly answer to what we liked or didn't like, and what we wanted to be when we grow up. Of course, when we were little we had no choice but to wait until we became adults. Now, we don't have that excuse.

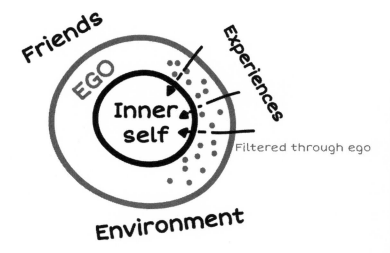

The strangest thing about the inner self is that it's not a separate entity from the ego. The inner self and the ego are two sides of the same coin, but whereas one reflects our internal world, feelings, and desires, the other mirrors the outer world. **Every experience coming from the outside is first filtered through our ego.** As a result, sometimes even straightforward events get interpreted rather particularly, happy occasions negatively, or unpleasant occurrences as something to be cheerful about.

We're all different, but we all have our internal triggers that make us uniquely valuable or less than desirable.

HARMONY OF THE EGO AND THE INNER SELF

In human history this duality of the psyche was often recognized and many attempts made to find a balance. Yet the solution for an average person to leave the ego completely behind was always akin to stripping off their own skin.

> Harmony comes from
> the silence of the ego.

Religious devotees in many cultures spend the majority of their time interpreting the world based on their revered texts. When westerners join these closed communities, they describe the attainment of profound changes in their internal selves. The reason for this cathartic experience is that such environments pay little attention to the needs of the ego, and people from western cultures find that highly liberating and peaceful once they get accustomed to it.

Moving to a monastery or practicing constant meditation aren't the only ways to attain inner harmony. The key is mindfulness **(13)**. The reason our egos have such an unequal influence on our feelings is because their overstimulated and get too much attention.

If we wanted to compare the identity of a Buddhist monk to a Hollywood celebrity, we'd see the difference as something like this:

Buddhist monk

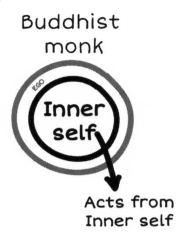

Acts from Inner self

Hollywood celebrity

Acts from Ego

The everyday life of a Buddhist monk is not skewed by the manifestations of the ego, which remains under-stimulated and cannot grow. The life of a celebrity in a western society is, however, the exact opposite. The amount of impulses that bombard a person who lives their life in front of the public eye leaves very little room for quiet self-reflection, and so the person must always play certain roles. A public person has little chance to live and express their true feelings since the ego determines how to act and with whom to connect.

Nevertheless, suppressing the ego can't be the solution because it acts like a child: if we forbid one thing, the urge to act out comes out in another way. **So, the ego learns just as a child does, through living example**. We can learn from others who have found true harmony in life, be it an ally or an adversary.

Creating harmony begins with attention and staying in the present. It's important to experience everything to its fullest in our lives. In such a condition it's clearly noticeable that colors become more vivid, sounds more distinct, tastes more intense, and conversations more engaging.

To maintain this mindset in everyday life is rather challenging because the outside world always tries to cater to our egos, pitting them against us and constantly calling for attention.

We have to find the time and place for advancement, either with a book, a place, or a friend that can help us to leave the trappings of the daily grind behind and engage with our core being.

THE MIRROR EFFECT

Blaming others brings up the problem of **self-reflection: being able to recognize our own failings**. If we don't make mistakes, we've got nothing to learn. And if we can't learn, we're unable to advance and be better in our team.

In the midst of our team members we should be able to safely come face-to-face with our mistakes without bringing the ego into it.

"Seeing the splinter in the eyes of others but missing the plank in the eye of oneself"
(Old Hungarian proverb)

Seeing the errors in others is easy, but finding them in ourselves is quite difficult, because the ego does a great job of explaining them away. When we examine the negatives in other people, we should first make a list of those attributes, then compare it with the faults we honestly find in ourselves. We'll soon realize that they're the same, and **what we find so annoying in others are the very things we avoid facing in ourselves (14)**. This is called channeling, or projecting.

In school there was a little boy who constantly teased his classmate about his big ears. He called him names in front of everybody. The teased classmate indeed had ears that stuck out a little, but nobody had noticed it previously until his teasing classmate called it out. What was his motivation? He himself was insecure about his own ears sticking out.

Everybody has the power to change themselves and to choose to take other people's advice. Conversely, most of us relish in doling out great tips of self-improvement, but have a hard time recognizing how little relevance these have on the lives of others. But when we look into the mirror and face up to the fact that some sort of change must take place, it's a lot more effective, because the realization comes from a deep understanding of our own situation.

Therefore, the most effective way to discover the root cause of problems in a team is to **encourage self-assessment among the team members**. This, however, requires strong discipline and the ability to self-reflect.

My ego doesn't allow me to admit
"I also have big ears"
because ego interprets this as a failing

THE GOAL OF SELF IN LIFE

What are our life plans? This premise has been the source of thousands of books, philosophical theses, and most of us raise this question at least once in our lives, if not daily.

It's quite easy for most of us to deduce that a singular goal in life cannot be to become rich, successful, or popular.

People at death's door—if they have a chance—almost always mention that the most cherished moments in their lives are times that somehow connected them with loved ones and people close to them. The single common theme in these stories is that they're tied to other people and not to objects.

Career, eSports, or dedication to a cause all provide suitable **frameworks** for our chosen lives. Small successes and great victories on a chosen path don't mean much on their own. They give no more than momentary joy. Success, money, and basking in attention are similar to a **canvas** on the frame. But ultimately it is always up to us what ends up getting on the canvas because we're the **painters** of our lives.

This is why wealth and popularity alone won't provide emotional satisfaction; only the things that from a 50-year distance can still give the feeling of joy and sense of accomplishment have any value to us. The people who surround us hold the key to true value in life.

7

SENSING

We're in the present when all of our senses and thoughts focus on our momentary situation and surrounding environment.

Surprisingly, people are hardly ever in that state of mind. As soon as we wake up, our mind starts going over the day's tasks and we immediately find ourselves somewhere else in our head. At night, lying in bed, we may stress about how we could've handled some conflict differently with a teammate, instead of letting our body drift to sleep. During a weekday we fantasize about a hike we plan on doing during the weekend, and while hiking we're thinking about work **(15)**.

If we live in the past or fantasize about the future, we lose the present.

HOW DO WE KNOW THAT WE'RE IN THE PRESENT?

When we experience the present, all of our senses fully engage with our surroundings and if something forms a thought or feeling in our head, we simply acknowledge that before letting it go. So, for example, if we step out into the street, we smell the air, see the traffic and the people around us, and feel the rhythm of our steps and the traction of our feet. When a thought comes over us, we just gently let it wash over like a wave and then allow it to pass. With diligent practice, almost any activity can be experienced this way. But to gain the necessary expertise, the most ideal method is to sit quietly while taking stock of all our senses one by one: seeing, hearing, smelling, tasting, feeling, and thinking. This is actually the most ancient technique of Buddhist meditation, called Vipassana.

In practice, if we play a match and stay in the present, we notice that suddenly all events are more clearly registered and we can easily understand our opponents' intents. Time slows down—as if our characters movements have switched to slow motion—and emotions of any kind, whether fear of losing or feelings of animosity toward our opponents, simply fall away. We don't think about the past or the future. We see our characters more clearly, understand our teammates' communication more succinctly, and sense our hand controls more precisely. Suddenly, we feel as if a giant veil has been dropped from the world around us.

Playing in such a state of mind has a positive impact on body and mind. With the lack of usual stresses, like worry and excitement, the reaction time shortens and the body becomes less fatigued.

WHAT INHIBITS US FROM STAYING IN THE PRESENT?

In a normal hour, several thousand thoughts can cross through our minds. The ego can't really exist in a quiet mind.

We can observe that in general we rarely like to be in silent, low-intensity environments. And even when we do, our mind starts moving in every direction, to the past or the future.

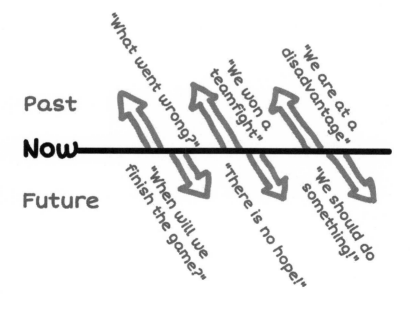

Children are different. When they play, they can completely engage with their world. If they imagine a castle, all its features and all the characters in it are fully developed and richly decorated.

In a child's mind, everything is real, even things they know to be pure fantasy.

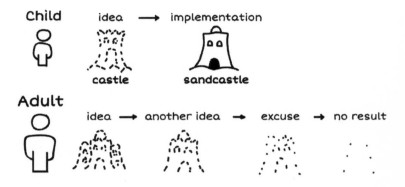

To be in the present means being fully conscious of the things we do. Many people use meditation, a short nap, taking a break, or doing some sort of exercise to find their way back to the now. When children build a sand castle, they can completely immerse themselves in the process of creation. A renowned research psychologist describes such a condition as the "flow" (Csikszentmihalyi, 1991).

BACK TO THE NOW

It's not possible to think of nothing by thinking about it. In fact, it's almost impossible to be free of thoughts for more than a couple seconds.

You can't stop thinking
with thoughts

Listen, relax,
let the flow happen

In lieu of meditation, there is a way to get back to the present with five minutes of relaxation or by washing our head with some cold water.

First we have to sit in a quiet place or create a relaxing atmosphere by playing some calming music through a headset.

Let's begin by breathing slowly. We can mentally observe as our chest is rising and sinking. Next, examine our palms and the back of our hands. Slowly raising our glance, let's observe our immediate environment next. What are the objects surrounding us? What are their colors and materials; what details make them significant or noticeable. Without hurry, let's take stock of all this.

If we're prior to a competition, we should accept that we're nervous, as it is natural and necessary to make us more alert and helps us perform at a higher level. We can consciously recognize our alert state of mind and mentally observe its effect on the mind and body. Let's welcome this feeling as a friend who has come to help us.

With each breath, we get more relaxed and feel lighter. We observe the people next to us, their motions and their facial expressions.

Let's watch the world around us with a child's eye, as if we're seeing everything for the first time. Our minds will take mental notes without any preconceptions.

EXPERIENCING THE FULL SPECTRUM

Before a match begins, many teams voice the mantra, "Let's focus." The question is, focus on what?

On our characters, the map at large, or on the opponents? There is tons of information at the beginning of the game and it is hard to process, so what's best to focus on?

Most teams reconcile this contradiction by beginning with concentration on their own tasks and shutting out the all the external events. In a stressful situation this strategy seems like a logical step because it lessens the chance of making mistakes.

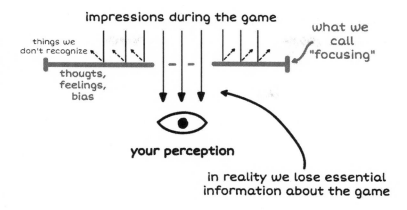

Yet experience shows that this sort of singularly-focused behavior closes out essential information and creates prejudiced attention.

Research psychologists of Harvard University (Most, Simons, Scholl, & Chabris, 2000) *proved in an experiment that if our brain is assigned to perform a specific and focused task, it can selectively filter out some glaringly obvious information in the task's immediate surroundings. In this experiment, the test subjects were asked to watch a video about people throwing balls back and forth, and count the number of tosses. The majority of subjects were able to recall the exact number of ball tosses after watching the video. Yet, when asked, they didn't notice anything unusual, even though a man in a gorilla suit waddled right into the middle of the ball players. This experiment showed that the brain is capable of completely blocking out external events when intensely focusing on something specific.*

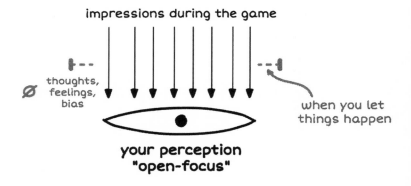

impressions during the game

thoughts,
feelings,
bias

when you let
things happen

your perception
"open-focus"

It is therefore important to allow ourselves to perceive the widest range of impressions during the beginning of the game. Nevertheless, we shouldn't force our attention to quickly scan from one thing to another because it will cause us to become fatigued quite early in the game. Rather, we should allow the many stimuli to reach our senses in parallel with each other. While we watch the map and the different players, we ought to just quietly take in the events. Children have the natural ability to observe without preconceived notions, but by the time we reach adulthood, our prejudices and internal monologue assign a tag to virtually any subject, person, or situation.

Besides, many other things can divert our attention, like mistakes made by us or our teammates, and the different levels or scores. When the mind wanders, it's easy to lose track of the game, and after a while even the narrowly-focused attention isn't present either.

We don't have to pay conscious attention to the course of events. We sometimes turn on the TV to watch an episode of a favorite series but become preoccupied with something else. When this happens, before we know it, the show is over and we can't recall a thing from it. But if we watch it again another time, we already know that we saw that episode and can remember specific details in it.

When we play and have to split our attention, we must deploy the same curiosity to know what's happening in the game. Such a **need** and **relaxed state of mind** assure that we receive the necessary information. Even if a large part of that acknowledgement subconsciously registers.

The two levels of our mind, the conscious and subconscious, can together process a tremendous amount of information, so why use only one or the other and not both?

DECISION MAKING AND SCHEMES IN GAME

Based on what's been stated previously, all the received information—at the conscious and subconscious level—can only be effectively processed if, beside our deliberate actions, we trust our unconscious or intuitive decision-making.

Nevertheless, it could still often happen that the intentional and intuitive choices contradict each other because the ego questions or overrides the wisdom of the subconscious. This defeatist questioning attitude is what's generally called self-doubt.

During the game or even in life, **primary intuitions** are decisions made by our subconscious **(16)**. They usually appear without delay in response to a given situation.

Thoughtful deliberation takes time, and in critical situations when every second counts, **intuition takes a leading role**.

Many times, we try to comply with set guidelines that we give to ourselves or receive from our teammates. "Next time in a situation X, I will do Y." Naturally, by doing this we rob ourselves the chance to choose because the decision is already made, and our intuition isn't allowed to take its role in the process. These handicaps seldom help a player so should be avoided at all cost.

SCHEMES

During the game, the individual players and commonly the team must make several deliberate decisions that break the flow and lead to diverging paths.

Professional players, therefore, consciously focus on reducing the number of divergences. For them, every situation offers two equally obvious options that they must choose from.

The reason for the possible options to be so few is because during preparation the team spends a large amount of time examining all possibilities of what works in any given situation. This practices what's best described as selective elimination.

The other method is working out the separate schemes for a character's reaction, for example, when choosing a path of escape or properly sequencing the utilized skills. These rules of thumb help the player give complex responses in many situations.

Enthusiastic Beginners

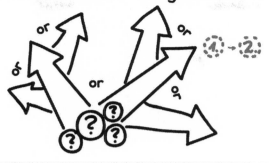

Veteran Professionals

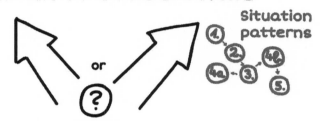

Situation patterns

**simple decision
with complex outcome**

The game of chess is a good example of where the professional players not only analyze each game piece's moving options, but learn hundreds, if not over a thousand, combinations of such options. These combinations mean that the player recognizes the outcome of a certain layout of the game pieces and knows the best moves to counter it or take advantage of it. In the professional world of chess, players are ranked by Elo score—named after the Hungarian born American physician Árpád Élő—and a pro is normally somebody who scores at least two thousand, whereas a grand master is above 2200. What's fascinating is that the Elo score *grades the knowledge of combinations. A beginner who knows around ten combinations is rated around 1200 to 1400, somebody with a hundred combinations gets 1600 to 1800, and a thousand combos is where the realm of professionals begin.*

The same way, in eSports, recognition of combinations appears, and these combinations are then automatically retained in the player's memory. The more often players meet the same situation, the more complex a series of responses they can produce. These firm responses can also be developed for predetermined conditions prior to live matches. We can record the answer for a situation, which afterwards is tried out during practice games. It's the same as if we changed the key combinations on our keyboards. The new setup may be more optimal, but it still takes time to get used to the new layout.

The advantage of thinking in combinations is that it eliminates the need to make minor decisions. For example, if there is only about a second of available time to react, a previously-learned response can automatically move the player forward, whereas trying to consciously choose would take too much time.

ONE STEP AHEAD OF THE ADVERSARY

In soccer, researchers have analyzed what a striker is paying attention to when trying to take a ball that is passed to a defending player. The interesting conclusion was that the attacking player barely watches the ball but closely observes the defender's legs and lower abdomen. We could say they try to read the opponent's "mind" and stay one step ahead of them (McDowall, 2011).

In eSports it's very important to follow the adversaries' moves and try to estimate their next steps. Professional teams usually have an easy time against inexperienced ones because they can come up with better drafts and neutralize the opposing teams' efforts. The pro teams can almost read the amateurs like an open book, even if they've never met them before. Experienced teams can come up with unique combinations and seemingly mystifying solutions that dominate their green opponents in many situations.

HOPE INSTEAD OF FEAR

There are two types of teams that exist before a game. One that is filled with **hope** and full of anticipation, and another that is overwhelmed by **dread** and with a sense of foreboding.

Excitement and nervousness are normal feelings in a live event where the teams and spectators can practically reach out and touch each other. The two opposing teams have the same exact goal but have very different emotions. So, what's going to happen?

Both teams make mistakes, and every misstep is an opportunity for the adversary. The team that is scared of losing, even if it notices the other's mishap, will not act on it. The team, on the other hand, which has a positive outlook and an attacking posture, will pounce on the chances that the opponents give and achieve an ever-widening lead.

Hope—the expectation of a positive outcome—represents the fact that opportunities always arise, but that one has to be mentally ready to reap their benefits.

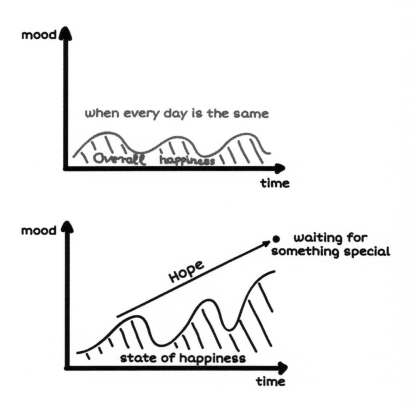

SIMPLICITY

In eSports, our best friends are a good foundation and well-practiced movements. These are integral parts of an e-Athlete that can be summoned with the "eyes closed."

Over-complicated tactics and combinations usually reduce the effectiveness of a team because all the extra thinking lowers the quality of delivery. Precise execution requires simplicity and an ample amount of practice.

Many people think that simple combinations are easy to figure out and effortlessly countered. But if they're delivered fast, by the time the opponent thinks about responding, it's already too late. Fast reaction can only occur against a combination if it's thoroughly practiced. If the opponent has to think, they won't have the time to act.

Leading teams will deliberately use simple but practical tactics against novices because they know that even if they are familiar with the given combinations, they will be unprepared to do anything against them.

The best boxers in the world were famous for certain combination of jabs and for their fancy footwork. Their opponents first and foremost tried to learn these tactics before their turn in the ring. Everybody did their homework. Yet, in the heat of the battle, when the punches were flying and the exhaustion started to set in, all the thoughts and learned countermeasures fell to the wayside. There was only time to think once lying on the floor – after the knockout.

SMALL SIGNS AND COINCIDENCES

How many times have the words "if only" been uttered in contests? The cold fact in eSports is that there is only one best. The winning team can be sure that even the happenstance worked in its favor. That's the team that does everything in sync in a hard-to-explain way that ultimately leads to final victory.

The question is: can we turn Lady Luck to be on our side? Is it even possible?

Let's remember that in eSports we choose a goal that's almost entirely outside of our influence. So, we need external help to reach our target, and we need our opponents to assist with that.

This can be best realized if we pay attention to small signs that occur during a game or between matches. If we're able to catch those seemingly insignificant signals, we can use them as markers. The more of these incidental occurrences we can find, the better we get at tuning into them. Eventually, we can get good enough to integrate them into our decision-making process and follow the path that is open to us.

But if winning is all about taking advantage of lucky coincidences, why bother preparing at all? The significance of preparation conditions the participant to have a long-term sense of experience and resolve during the event, which assures success. If that feeling is missing, it's hard to accomplish anything in the long run. Preparation breeds confidence for the team, which is indispensable, because as the saying goes, luck favors the prepared.

8

EMOTIONS

We can display a wide array of feelings, and several of them are typically present in an e-Athlete.

- ☐ Anger or rage
- ☐ Disappointment
- ☐ Frustration
- ☐ Fear
- ☐ Resignation, capitulation
- ☐ Excitement
- ☐ Joy
- ☐ Satisfaction
- ☐ Self-confidence
- ☐ Resolve
- ☐ Happiness
- ☐ Hope

All of the above feelings are rather forceful, inhibit our logical thinking, and force our train of thought inwards.

If feelings take a hold on us, we may suddenly notice that we have a death grip on the mouse or our body posture becomes close and defensive.

This condition is generally described as being overwhelmed by emotions. The term is quite descriptive because when we feel this way, whether incredibly positive or negative, time seems to stand still and we sense it as a whole-body experience. We quite literally surrender ourselves to the feeling.

WHERE ARE FEELINGS COMING FROM?

Emotions are arising from our own thoughts or as a reaction to an external event. How it begins depends on the individual who experiences it.

For example, losing a match or making a mistake can bring up emotions such as anger, rage, fear, or dread. Physiologically, a small part of our brain, the amygdala, generates certain impulses that prepare the body to react to a supposed outside attack and divert most of the dissolved oxygen toward the muscles instead of the brain. Ironically, in eSports this is the time when the brain especially needs the extra oxygen to resolve a problem.

When **feeling threatened**, most of the time we get angry, which **shuts down the path toward creativity and logical thinking**. To an outside spectator we seem to act irrationally.

Our emotions and the experience of their depths have their origin in our upbringing. We learn from our parents how to react to certain situations. Children clearly sense their parents' nervousness and remember both the circumstances that brought this on and how they reacted.

By the time we reach adulthood, we have a hard time separating cause from effect. We simply settle it in our head that "clumsiness makes us mad," "helplessness gets us frustrated," or "loss causes us to feel sorrow." Yet we can't consciously explain the origins of these feelings; we just say this is who we are. **We react childishly to many situations even as adults because we've learned to act that way as children**. Except, if we had a chance to reexamine most of these events and our responding mental processes as adults for the first time, we'd probably react to them entirely differently.

In eSports being angry or sad following a lost game isn't caused by the fact that we were beaten. The roots originate from a much earlier experience, for example, when we first disappointed our parents by bringing home a bad grade and we were scolded, or when we were made fun of by our peers for being clumsy.

The best method to understand our emotions is to examine how we react to an event and ask ourselves the question: is this the only way I can react? People, for example, who can vocally state in the middle of their episode of anger that they are upset, are a lot more aware of their emotions and have made the first important step to facing them.

WHO OWNS THE EMOTION?

When a feeling rises up in us, we unconsciously link it to a person, place, object, or event that seemingly caused it. The danger is that such a presumed link will result in automatically assigned blame.

Positive and negative feelings both work by this sort of mechanism. But it also means that **we prefer to be with**

people whom we relate to with positive emotions, and often without consciously thinking about that.

In reality, **our emotions are entirely our own creations, independent of who or what caused them (17)**.

Feeding positive emotions is as possible as expressing our personality through words. But because negative feelings are more enduring, it's quite possible that as children we learned many more instances of expressing negative emotions. Regardless, the way we describe other people will determine our relation to them.

When a player sees the outside world in a positive light, they consider encountering their adversaries as opportunities to learn and their lost games as life lessons. Yet these people are often viewed as uninteresting.

There are also players with strong opinions who voice disparaging remarks about the opposing teams and are always ready to point out who caused a lost game. Still, these people receive plenty of attention and their remarks are welcomed by others.

Despite all this, in the long run, the team members choose to gravitate toward the player with the positive attitude because they also feel charged up around them, more so than around someone who just drains their energy with constant negativity.

EXPERIENCING OR SUBDUING EMOTIONS

When it comes to feelings, there are two types of people: those who learned to control them from childhood, and the ones who allow themselves to wear their heart on their sleeve.

Although holding back our feelings has its own drawback, too. They **become a thorn** in our soul. These feelings, over and over, come to the surface in recurring situations, only because they couldn't be worked out in the first place. Positive feelings that are held back could produce the same effect if they aren't shared. They rob the person who otherwise had a part in it from experiencing the joy it has caused.

Constantly muzzled emotions can cause physical problems as well; they can bring discomfort, pain, or even illness to the person. We can relate to this feeling when we fight against something very strongly; eventually we feel sick from the thought of doing it.

Expressing our emotions is very important because an overwhelming feeling—as its name suggests—can be a hard task to handle if not done consciously. And losing control means also losing the chance to make proper decisions.

If we constantly let our feelings come to the surface, they will spread naturally. The best analogy is sunshine. If it shines evenly, it warms without much damaging effect. But if it's focused with a magnifying glass, it will burn the targeted surface.

BETWEEN MATCHES

The short breaks (5-10 minutes) between games are only enough to take care of our most basic needs. This time allows us to empty our minds (and bladders) and refocus our attention for the next game. This can be particularly difficult if we just came out of a grueling round.

When the head is filled with the emotions of being upset over a lost game or joy from a great victory, it's hard to stay in the present. And if we aren't in the present, it's difficult to stay engaged and prepare for what's coming next. We can hardly say that we're focused and ready for the upcoming round while being overwhelmed by feelings of all sorts.

Having a sense of closure and acceptance is a necessary process that helps to enter the next match feeling anew.

ACCEPTANCE

People generally aren't open to change because it's in our human nature to follow familiar patterns and be comforted by them. We even tend to constantly repeat the same mistakes because that's the process we know and it influences our daily habits. We get upset and know that we should do things differently. Yet, particularly when we dwell on the past, we lose sight of the present task at hand, and instead stay occupied with things that don't even exist anymore.

Interestingly, **players can come around much faster after winning a game than following being soundly beaten,** the latter causing a drawn-out period of somber mood.

Based on the psychological research of Ledgerwood et al. (Ledgerwood & E. Boydstun, 2014), people spend significantly more time in a state of loss than in a state of winning.

People have a hard time switching negative thoughts to positive. If I had a dozen candies and I offered somebody three of them, the person would rightly think that I'm a generous person. But if I took out the same dozen candies, put them on the table, took nine of them away and then told that same person to take what's left, I would look really stingy.

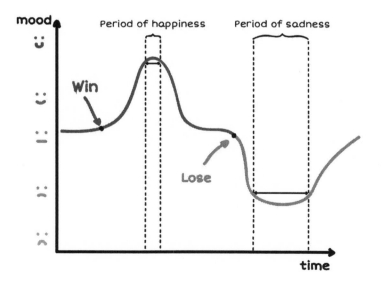

Negativity, however, doesn't solve anything, and it just gnaws on the person carrying such thoughts. The only way to break free is by accepting what has happened and finding closure.

Acceptance can also become a reflex even in significant life events. The trick is to properly apply such methods even in the most difficult situations.

STAGES OF GRIEF

The Kübler-Ross model (Kübler-Ross, 2009) can be perfectly applied for feelings that come up after a lost eSports game. It aptly describes the different stages of emotion during that time.

Denial   **Anger**   **Bargaining**   **Depression**   **Acceptance**

Denial - The first emotion that surfaces after losing an important game is denial. When we experience this stage, we mentally shut down and don't allow any outside information to enter even if it is important to continue.

"I can't believe it!"
"This can't happen to me."
"It can't be true."

Anger - When angry, we push away everybody around us. We blame everybody and everything around us, and our ego is truly hurt.

"Leave me alone!"
"I can't stand you!"

Bargaining - During bargaining, we believe that we can change the outcome by offering a deal or promise of some sort. Of course, the past cannot be undone.

"Maybe if I practiced more."

Depression - Emptiness reigns and nothing makes sense anymore. The inevitable is realized and we feel utterly helpless. The world closes in on us and we want solitude. The only solace in this stage is that it is as the others. It will pass and no words can change it or make it go away faster.

"I don't want to be part of this team anymore!"

Acceptance and reprocessing - The turning point occurs when we finally find closure and get over what transpired. What follows may not be the perfect situation, but we have new hope, find renewed goals, and are able to get up and start on a new path.

"We can focus on the next game."
"There is nothing to lose!"

CONSCIOUS ACCEPTANCE

The stages of acceptance normally happen this way. For some people it takes a certain amount of time, but for others it may take longer.

Dealing with a lost game, on the other hand, doesn't allow a player to work through the whole gamut because quite often there is only a 10-minute break between rounds.

So, when we understand that consciously accepting what has happened is a matter of **deliberate decision**, then we can control the issue about time **(18)**.

First we must think of the fact that failing is human and it's up to us to get up and continue after a fall. When a child falls, we do best by them if, instead of focusing on the trauma, we divert their attention to something more remote. The crying stops as soon as they become interested.

A similar strategy works for us too after a loss. The importance of deliberate focus becomes apparent when we pivot out of emotionally responding to what just transpired and start to think forward with a cool head.

We first have to accept our emotional state and give room to our feelings while taking a step back and observing the situation almost as an outsider. If we can remain objective, we're already in better shape. For example, if we lose the first game at a prestigious international event, we can remind ourselves that we always dreamed of being here and now we are. The key is to view the given situation from a **different perspective**, and be a good parent to our thoughts as we would be to a crying child.

Once the ego goes quiet, our emotions will calm too, and we can start weighing new options. We have a free choice to accept what happened or return to self-pity, which is the ego's favorite occupation. If we choose to accept the facts, then we can congratulate our opponents and, with this gesture, we find closure. But this is also the point where we start considering our next round.

Let's not forget: the emphasis is on conscious acceptance.

The worst that could happen is if we hold back our feelings and use up all of our energy to keep them bottled in until they finally come out with a burst to the surface.

Conscious acceptance is similar to a clean canvas that's taken out by a painter. If there were something already on the canvass, it would have an influence on what appeared on it in the future.

BARRIERS

Emotional barriers are mental blocks that are lodged into our psyches over the years. Healthy and emotionally properly developed children are usually very open about their feelings and always ready to express them, whether good or bad.

Yet in some families, showing emotions is considered a sign of weakness. In those homes, the parents instill in their children that crying in front of others is somehow improper, which only builds invisible emotional barriers in them.

These psychological blocks later inhibit the affected individuals as adults from fully experiencing their emotions, both joys and sorrows, because those feelings remain bottled up and their existence denied. Then it happens to those seemingly even-keeled individuals that years later they break down sobbing from immense emotion. When this occurs, it's quite likely that their emotional barrier just came down.

People bottle up their emotions like children fill up their buckets in a sandbox. If they pack them full, soon they realize that carrying around heavy and full buckets is too much work, so they turn them over. Grown people are a lot less sensible about their bottled up feelings and lug them around for a long time, hoping that one day they will magically disappear.

We can imagine that if our feelings were always expressed like a river is allowed to flow in its natural state, they would often overwhelm anything in their close proximity.

Channeling and regulating our emotions is important because, instead of being a destructive and unbridled force, they can encourage us and give us the extra boost we need to accomplish our goals.

FACING FEELINGS HONESTLY

One important element of harmony is honesty, particularly honesty toward ourselves.

Many people think that it's a bad thing to reveal our feelings. As adults, we may still remember how our grandparents showed their displeasure when we did something mischievous as small kids. Thinking back, we probably just smile and know that their anger was most likely justified.

Their furor also quickly dissipated and didn't leave a lasting thorn in us. Yet, the reason we still remember the event and our grandparents' reactions is because they worked as corrective actions and played their part to help us in becoming upstanding citizens.

Honesty is an important factor when it works internally to set our course. When we're honest with ourselves, we are able to take a step back and examine our thoughts and actions from a certain distance, which helps to reevaluate their validity.

Having honest feelings means that we face up to their existence despite what others say. If we're able to stay true to our emotions, then our actions also appear valid to people around us and they can surely consider us genuine and trustworthy.

EXPERIENCING EMOTIONS

Being conscious about our feelings gives us the opportunity to choose how to express them.

Let's take the example of rage; how do we deal with that?

1. Destructively – slam our hands to the table or break something
2. Yell at others – although not angry at a particular person, their presence and any small infraction are a good excuse
3. Go training – release pent up energy through rigorous exercise

If we're able to consciously recognize our feelings, we can choose in what shape or form we will display them.

The same goes for happiness. When we enjoy a sudden victory, we automatically want to share it with others. When we finally succeed after a long struggle, get a diploma, or receive a great promotion, we act like an e-Athlete who has just become a champion. We pump the air with our fist, give high fives, and jump into the arms of others.

And there are, of course, the types of people who are so removed from their own feelings that they direct their emotions completely toward others, such as their team members or opponents. They can be recognized by the constant stream of gossip that comes from their mouths.

Considering that they expend their emotions on other people who are out of earshot, what is the net effect of their effort? In truth, **gossiping has the greatest detriment on the person who is spreading it**.

RECOGNIZING THE EMOTIONS OF OTHERS

If we're able to identify the exact feelings of others and receive their messages—for example, when being called out for not playing good enough—then we can decide on the best way to react to them.

First we must establish that every emotion that rises up in a person belongs to that person alone. Regardless of somebody being mad at us during a match, that feeling is in them. This is an important fact to recognize because the player who's too busy having an emotional breakdown during a match **cannot focus on the possible options and outcomes of the game, but instead is preoccupied by their internal turmoil**.

After making all the mistakes, every player has a choice to turn the outcome of the game around by making the right moves next time.

If we become influenced by our teammate's or opponent's feelings, we will reinforce their effect in thought and action. **Feelings give birth to thoughts, which bring forth actions that ultimately influence our very reality.**

Many players feed their negative thoughts and emotions because of their own egos. The aim of the ego is to elevate the individual, and it's most effectively done through negativity, just like in the evening news that is most highly watched. Our psyche has an ingrained negative bias and it's typical for almost all age groups (other than children) and for most cultures. From an evolutionary point of view, this bias has served us well in the past, because it helped us to prepare ahead, but accepting that unconditionally is a trap.

POLARIZED EMOTIONS

Finally, let's examine emotions in a different light.

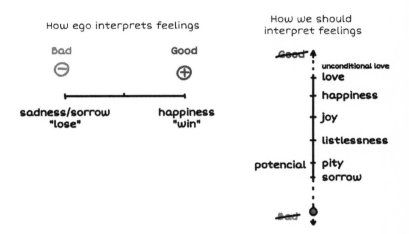

The human ego interprets feelings on opposite extremes. There are positive and negative emotions. All emotions are placed either on the negative or the positive pole. This, however, is subjective, because often the same feeling is negative for one person and positive for another.

The ego operates quite simply: to label the behavior of people.

There is another approach that is called the **thermometer model**, which instead places emotions on a scale based on how energizing they are. All emotions have a level of "heat," as some are hot and others are cold.

The basic idea of the model is that there are no better or worse feelings when they're compared to one other; they're only measured by their respective levels of energy. And when we master our emotions and not the other way around, we can create our reality through them.

TEAM HUDDLE, MATCH ASSESSMENT

Let's consider a common occurrence in a team's day: a team meeting. If the purpose of this meeting is to analyze a match and learn from its conclusions, then we'll have to keep in mind the following:

1. Keep the discussion factual and to the point while staying focused on the specifics
2. Consider the game objectively as if we watched another team play. The characters are discussed without naming the actual members who controlled them.
3. The moderator of the discussion must curtail any personal attacks and leveling of blame. These are counterproductive.
4. Pay attention to the person speaking, as it helps in understanding their motives and the points of view of others.
5. All speakers should focus on constructive solutions and finish with a suggestion or alternative option.

If these points are observed during the discussion, then the emotional pitfalls are avoided that would otherwise make the meeting counterproductive.

NEGATIVE ATTITUDE DURING GAMES

Being pessimistic can have a negative effect on the game. When this happens, we feel threatened or disappointed, and it overpowers us to the point that we lose faith in the game. This occurs precisely because we believe in ourselves so much when the match begins, but find our hopes are dashed when the situation changes. We feel this way and can't provide an answer to find a different outcome.

When we fall in a hole of negative emotions, it affects our manner of communication. Our tone of voice becomes flat, statements are replaced by sharp orders, and as the game deteriorates, we get increasingly frustrated, start to blame others, or simply fall silent.

Negative attitude is like a self-fulfilling prophecy; we project forward our internal defeat to the eventual outcome. There is, however, a way to combat this.

There are two basic types of athletes. The first one is a born talent who believes that everybody has certain potentials, but being exceptional is a privilege and it is unique. The second type believes in hard work and focuses on honing their skills and strengths at a constant rate. These two athletes experience loss completely differently. The latter processes a lost game more simply **without considering it detrimental**, and assesses the outcome as a lesson to reach a higher level next time. Somebody who is born talented, on the other hand, views loss as a shocking indictment on their very being as not good enough.

It's important to keep faith in ourselves and in our team. Simply said, we must always put pride in our work and give a hundred percent even when the chance of winning is no more than 1%.

Instead of worrying about what others do, we should focus on our own tasks, and if things are hard to do alone, then let's get help. Allowing our mouth to run freely during a game is a bad habit and the same energy can be used to perfect our moves or help our teammates. Teams that pull together during difficulties are better equipped to get over a lost game and rebound faster.

A THORN INSIDE; LET'S OPEN UP!

Inside the life of a team or another type of community there are always things that are left unsaid in the daily bustle. Sometimes it's easier to glaze over things or sweep them under the rug than to stop the daily flow and get into confrontations over something minor. Yet these small annoyances stay inside us as irritating thorns.

When these emotional thorns get deeply enough embedded, we unconsciously start to dislike the person and maintain a constant low-level hostility toward them. Even though we attempt to ignore it, this sort of unexamined animosity is the source of many spoiled relationships between people.

The truth is, everybody makes mistakes and has some annoying habits. Yet they're hardly ever detrimental, and they're easier to accept out in the open when we find the proper format and venue to deal with them.

In everyday practice, when the proper time is set aside to deal with interpersonal issues, it should be done privately if it's between two people or in front of the whole team when discussed in general. Constructive criticism has a way of lifting people up by offering methods to improve. It's also the source of the basic premise that a person can be only improved if they have the understanding and willingness (and not the resistance) to improve themselves.

9

THOUGHTS

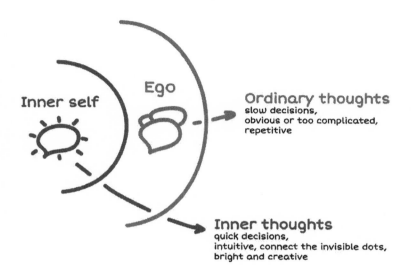

Inner self

Ego

Ordinary thoughts
slow decisions,
obvious or too complicated,
repetitive

Inner thoughts
quick decisions,
intuitive, connect the invisible dots,
bright and creative

THOUGHTS CAN TAKE DIFFERENT PATHS

GENERAL OR EGO-DRIVEN THOUGHTS

We can separate two types of thought processes. The first one we can describe as general or ego-driven. These are the webs of internal monologues that our brain spins around our daily activities or as a response to what's happening around us. When our ego reacts to something, the solution comes rather slowly because we weigh all options and possible outcomes against our current social standing and interpersonal relations. The chosen path is most often what we judge as the best at the given moment. Because almost all of these thoughts compare and contrast with our previously stored experiences, they're mostly based on recall or learned patterns. The decisions come as we're slowly deliberating the right course of action in a sort of autopilot.

INNER THOUGHTS

Inner thoughts and intuitions appear when our mind is free or if we face an extreme situation. While stressed or tired, these sorts of thoughts most often elude us despite our best intentions. On the other hand, when we're deeply involved with a subject or just have a clear mind, these creative inner thoughts come up to the surface seemingly out of nowhere. Their common characteristic is that they appear almost instantly in intuition as if a light bulb suddenly came on in our head.

If, for example, this thought is an answer sought to a problem, it may not seem logical at first because it doesn't match the patterns laid out with traditional thinking. This occurs because our intuitive thinking discovers such complex connections in a fraction of the time that it would normally require to think it through. Still, more often than not these inner thoughts are correct and eventually validated. **The inner thoughts are also characterized as being extremely creative and appear to be a leap from conventions,** such as when a scientist discovers a new theory that is only proved later to be correct after long examination.

For some people, the best time to think creatively is right before going to sleep. They even tend to keep a notepad on the nightstand to jot down and preserve their thoughts for the morning.

Similar to the inner self, inner thoughts appear when the ego is calm in the background and gives access to our deeper internal world where processes happen more freely and in more directions than on our disturbed and two-dimensional surface.

INTERNAL DISCOURSE

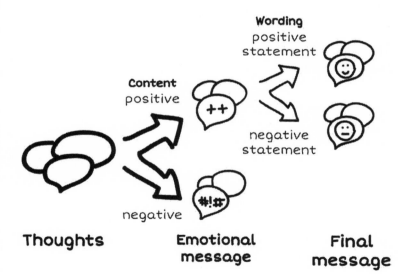

While participating in eSports, our mind is a swirling vessel of thoughts, and many such thoughts are just the creations of our ego. As a teammate, we quickly learn that maintaining a positive attitude and encouraging others in our group is necessary to preserve a healthy atmosphere. But this also goes for our thoughts.

If all we can think about is that we really suck, then even our encouragement comes out negative, like "let's try a little harder." When our internal feelings and external communication contradict each other, we lose the sense of authenticity. Even if we try to project an air of confidence, our gestures and body language reveal our true feelings. Our thoughts and emotions display our true character and at best we come across as somebody who's faking it at the moment; at worst, we're considered a disingenuous person in general.

When things don't happen in our favor or we simply aren't doing so well, we can't allow our emotions to deliver our efforts the final blow. We know exactly our abilities and how much and how well we practiced. Instead of feeling negative about ourselves, we should focus on turning things around with the ability that we previously gave to ourselves.

Encouraging ourselves and others is not only important to remind everyone of our true capabilities, but by fighting to the max until the very end, we have the chance to turn things around even at the last moment.

Our internal monologue has to be as much of a cheerleader as our fans and our coach who all believe in us until the very end are. If we project a different attitude, we are the first ones who let the whole team down.

POSITIVE AFFIRMATIONS

When we make statements to ourselves or others, we should do it from a positive direction, not by denying something negative.

Logically when we say, "I hope we play the best game tonight," and "I hope nothing's going to stop us from playing the best game tonight," we are technically saying the same thing.

Yet, it's the classic example of "don't think of an elephant" or the "white bear problem," (Wegner, Schneider, Carter, & White, 1987) which invariably conjures up the internal image of the respective fauna. While the positive statement immediately focuses on the ways to make our game the best, the negative begins by examining the traps we want to avoid.

So, instead of getting tuned to our goal, we see the objects that could inhibit us from getting to it.

Our mind works as if we could avoid seeing the images it creates.

The following are a few examples of how the mind perceives something and its true meaning.

The mind doesn't recognize the negative construct, so as a rule of thumb, it's better to formulate solution-oriented thoughts with the aim to nurture a positive attitude.

Positively charged thoughts are a matter of self-training, because just as people can fall back to pessimistic thoughts out of habit, they can also be changed to the other direction.

ENCOURAGING INNER THOUGHTS

When we recognize that we're using too many negative statements, we can change them by making a conscious effort to replace them with something that's the opposite.

The change, of course, is not going to be immediate, and at first it will be rather difficult to even catch. Most of our thoughts are formed seemingly automatically and are hard to get a handle on right at their source. Most of us can be accused of being lazy with our thoughts; however, this is not necessarily the case. If we experience something negative from another person, we assume an accusatory tone. When somebody else is critical toward us, we become defensive. These are all automatic reactions, just as being negative is, and so are initially hard to change because they're so ingrained into our personality.

The best strategy is to exchange a negative sentence with a positive one once in a while. We can't force a complete about-face in our attitude all at once, but by gradually changing it for something that we prefer, we can make it last.

Eventually we notice the negativity in other people, too. This happens because we become conscious of any sort of foul disposition, and it means that we're on the right path toward changing it in ourselves too.

It equally means that having a naturally positive outlook will become the norm for us. Our mind becomes instinctively tuned to making affirmative statements, whether expressing a feeling, assessing a situation, or considering an outlook. This creative behavior mobilizes hidden resources that come forth when needed.

Let's examine a few specific examples of expressions that we can tell ourselves or others:

1. "I can do this"
2. "I'm able to accomplish it"
3. "I will give it all"
4. "Winning or losing is secondary. What's important is that we put pride in our play."
5. "I will accomplish my dream"
6. "I will enjoy this game"
7. "I believe in you"

We should find the most suitable expressions that best describe our positive feelings and avoid negativity.

IS IT IMPORTANT, WHAT OTHERS THINK?

Other people's opinions often disturb us. We sense the ill feelings directed toward us, such as when they consider us clumsy after a bad day.

Most people pay attention to the opinions of others, and even though many of us state that we don't care about such a thing, our behavior shows otherwise. So, why is that?

People form opinions about others when they have an anchor point they can pivot from. If somebody is rich, young, beautiful, or rather bald, black, or kind, this can be the one principal attribute that is needed to layer all other qualities around it.

Human nature is such that we have a constant need to reevaluate ourselves and **compare with others**. This starts at a very young age as part of a natural process of socialization because all children thrive to be the center of attention. They learn it early that the best tactic to gain the awe of others is by being better at something than their peers. The ego demands the recognition of unique qualities in each and every person because it knows that it's the key to **gaining more attention**.

The superficial mind, or ego, considers other people's opinions as very important. It remains true even as we know that what others say has no bearing on us. Opinions are similar to emotions in that they only affect us if they're our own or if we identify with them.

Similar to a weather vane that always turns whichever direction the wind is blowing, people who take their cues from others can't ever accomplish anything significant. We should remember that negative opinions are mostly the outward projections of the scrutinizing person's inner misery. Constructive criticism, however, is as rare as it is valuable, because it helps with improvements that are apparent to an impartial outside observer.

The truth is, it matters not what other people think of us; **the only thing that's important is how we think about ourselves (19).**

10

WAKING UP AS A **WINNER**

CYCLES OF PERFORMANCE

Our ability to perform at peak level in a given match is cyclical. Weightlifters often encounter the phenomenon wherein they have the same muscle mass, their diet and energy levels are the same, and yet their performance level is nowhere near their usual best. We call this performance a cycle or wave **(20)**.

This term is quite descriptive because even though it's more or less independent of the athletes, the cycles are observable and predictable.

Minor peaks and valleys of performance are a daily occurrence and are in sync with a person's mood that changes from day to day. There are also weekly and bi-weekly fluctuations that indicate the athlete's general condition.

Such phenomena well match human nature, because everything is in constant flux in our environment. Change is in our surroundings as it is in our bodies.

The waves of changes propel advancement.

As we ride on waves, willing or not, sooner or later we find ourselves on a crest. The view from there may be a bit frightening but it is still thrilling.

In eSports, the player describes when this happens that things happen almost too easily, winning is a breeze, and a sense of invincibility comes to the surface.

When the opposite occurs, and the player suddenly finds themselves in a hole, overly harsh self-criticism is definitely not the right course action. Better concentration and more energy gets the participant through the same course, but what is a plus is that this is the time when the e-Athlete advances most in their skills.

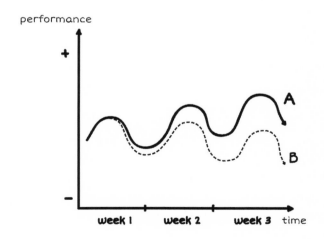

Investing more energy during training may not have the same effect, but once over the trough, this plus propels the player noticeably better in matches (A). On the other hand, without training, decreasing tendencies become the norm (B). The difference between continued training and the lack of it will be clearly apparent after just a matter of weeks.

THE LAST AFTERNOON

The last afternoon prior to competition should be spent resting and allowing the brain to relax while doing some sort of calming activity.

For e-Athletes, doing light physical exercises, watching a movie, or enjoying any pleasant activity is a perfect way to get distracted from thinking about the upcoming challenges.

Many people are under the false impression that even the last minutes should be used for preparation. Yet the truth is that if the necessary skills weren't honed during the practice period, then the last day won't make any difference either. On the other hand, a proper rest will help to perform optimally.

SLEEP AS PART OF PREPARATION

After a relaxing afternoon, the most important physiological necessity, sleeping, should be considered as a necessary part of preparation. During sleep, the body and mind switch to recuperation mode. Regular sleep of 7-8 hours is essential to wake up the next morning ready for the competition.

Two types of sleep patterns can be differentiated:

During NREM (Non-Rapid-Eye-Movement) the heart rate and breathing slow down significantly, and the body recharges the most effectively.

REM (Rapid-Eye-Movement) sleep is typified by involuntary eye movements and fast, shallow breathing. Sleep researchers call this the dream state.

DREAMS

Dreams have certain significance in our lives and even though many people claim that they don't dream, in reality they simply don't remember them after waking up (Hobson, Pace-Schott, & Stickgold, 2000).

Our dream world is often populated by fears, hopes, and unresolved conflicts left behind from our waking hours. By no coincidence, during more difficult periods in our lives, we have more frequent nightmares, because our mind is attempting to work through them by reliving those encounters. Yet those bad dreams aren't simply the slavish replays of prerecorded events; they're rather a combined construct of what happened and how it reflects in our psyche. Persons participating in our dreams take on significant roles equal to their importance in our real life, such as with the appearance of parents and other loved ones. Also, because dreams aren't bound by laws of physics nor linear time, the structure and storyline of these constructs have more to do with our psyche than with physical reality.

Still, experiences gained while dreaming have as much significance as the ones encountered during waking hours, except that they're processed differently by the conscious mind.

In our dreams, the ego is also more of a passive watcher than an active participant. It, however, interprets the dream and that's the version we remember when we wake up.

The purpose of dreaming is to organize, as well as generalize, our feelings or desires and apply our experiences. Our wishes often first take shape in our dream world, just as much as we can realize the subject of our daydreams, so dreaming and waking hours are closely tied together. Lucid dreaming, as a discipline of controlling our dreams, has a strong correlation with how well we can control our conscious desires.

THE ROLE OF THE E-ATHLETE ON D-DAY

As the day of the contest arrives, we wake with a nervous stomach even though we went to bed early the night before in order to get up rested.

We're burdened by the expectations put on us by our coach, teammates, and fans. We feel the significance of the day because we've been waiting for it to arrive.

In all honesty, such anxious thoughts only stress the e-Athlete and do more harm than good.

The best (and only thing) we can do on this day is to **give it all we've got**. The important thing is not to live up to the expectation of others, but to be able to look into the mirror the night after the competition and say, **"I did my very best."**

ROUTINES

Routines are mental tricks that help the competitor to better concentrate and tune into the upcoming event. The only thing that we need to watch out for with respect to routines is that they shouldn't become automatic, because then they would lose their intended purpose. For many e-Athletes, routines are morphed into obsessive compulsive behavior patterns or become a subject of superstition.

A few of these routines that are observed in the world of eSports:

1. The tight gripping of a hand warmer before a deciding match.
2. Saying a prayer or mantra before the game with the team.
3. Doing a signature move with a character at the beginning of the match.
4. Reading, one last time, a self-penned reminder.
5. Quickly mumbling the game plan one last time before starting.

There are routines too that aim to retrace the path that leads to a mistake, correct it, and recoup from there. For example, touching a virtual object on the course signals the mind about a new start.

Also, there are routines that remind the player to make a conclusion about what has just transpired.

The above are just a few examples, but they have the same familiar pattern that shows their users' intent of putting some thought into forming them. The number of repetitions varies for each routine, but normally it takes 12-20 occasions in different situations for each to become a standard routine. Once that happens, the routine makes the proper emotional connection.

The purpose of routines is to be used as a means to an end and not as tools to replace a missing skill set or crucial knowledge. Regular coffee drinkers use the bitter brew to wake up, but after a while they often consume two cups instead of one to get the same effect because of their built-up tolerance to caffeine. The same tolerance may be noticed to a set of routines with athletes, and when it becomes overwhelming, the person is labeled as severely superstitious or even suffering from OCD. So, if we know we can win without a specific routine, then it's time to drop it. As our habits and skills change we can always try out new ones that help with focus, warming up, or calming the nerves.

BEFORE EVERY GAME

Many teams have a set of routines to close a match and get prepared for the upcoming one in the time allowed. The following are a few examples of mental and practical routines.

- ☐ Getting refreshed – Bathroom break to wash face or getting some fresh air
- ☐ Clear the head – Closing the past match, putting aside the worries and focusing on the present

- ☐ Walk – Leaving the station and taking a walk to get the circulation going
- ☐ Energy replacement – Eating some easily digestible food and properly hydrating
- ☐ Tuning to each other – Many teams use a motto or a group cheer to get the right cohesion and achieve a common vibe.
- ☐ Game Plan – The team rehashes the practiced game plan, helping to recall the different points to be reached in the game. This serves as munition that helps to focus the team on the proper course. Chanting the game plan doesn't help the mind within the game; it only helps to calm the ego down before the event.

CALL OUTS AND RECALLS

There are short expressions that have direct associations or deeper meanings for team members. Depending on the person, some prefer to say them out loud or just in their head. These terms are mostly cryptic and easily identifiable by their users but rarely uttered without additional context in everyday conversations.

Some examples:

1. **Praise** – after a successful round or particularly good move, giving a compliment to self or to a team member ("Yes, that was outstanding!")
2. **Command** – when the heat of the action is driving the team ("Turn now!")
3. **Change** – when the current tactic isn't working and a complete change is required (Let's try something new!")

4. **Recall** – when a previously practiced move or tactic needs to be recalled for a teammate ("Go with the 'vacuum-echo' combination!")

BELIEVING IN OUR ABILITIES

If we know that we're sufficiently prepared to go against the best teams, then we have to believe in our abilities too. Physical and technical preparedness is not enough without mental readiness.

The latter is important to help our mind to have the confidence to utilize our full abilities during the contest. This sense of self-assurance assists in recalling all that was learned when we engaged in intense training sessions.

Don't believe in beating your opponent but believe in your own abilities

There are inexperienced teams that choke during a match or game, and the viewing public, along with the commentators, while watching this unfold, conclude that the team is still green. A few months later, after the team goes through intensive training, it's tested once more against a well-known team with similar abilities – and it loses again. The outside observers assume that the team didn't improve at all without seeing what has been happening in the **background**. The team, in fact, advanced quite a bit through ample amounts of practice, and its capabilities became more optimal. Nevertheless, in the match they couldn't deploy what they had learned during training. They simply lacked the necessary confidence to use the learned moves in a live contest. For this very reason the coaches remind their teams to "do as in training."

LEADER'S MOTIVATION

> If we lose today we continue until we
> become the best;
> if we win, then that day has already come.

The purpose of a motivational speech is to induce the proper emotions in the listeners and help them muster the extra effort necessary for winning. It is similar to warming up the muscles before a game, except motivational speeches warm up the mind.

> Most leaders don't know, they only
> assume, that they can motivate their
> players, which is already sufficient.

HUMMING CALMS THE NERVES

Some athletes when going into deep concentration forget to breathe and suddenly start to suffer from apnea. This may happen more often than one might think, even at top competitions, such as in the Olympic games.

What helps in an episode like that is if we take our mind off of the game. In the last nervous minutes, focusing on the tactics can result in the opposite effect, and not thinking about it is much more helpful. It's best to remember: our muscle memory already knows what to do.

One surefire method to draw our attention away from the tense final few minutes is to hum a favorite tune. Since humming is a focused activity and it regulates the breathing, it calms the nerves and gives the brain the extra oxygen it needs by forcing a deeper form of breathing. Perhaps even the people surrounding the performer will respond positively to such performance.

GET THE NEEDED PLUS OUT OF EXCITEMENT

If we feel that something is important to us, we often respond by becoming excited even if we feel calm in our head. Our bodies signal this excited state, and we have no other choice but to accept it as normal.

People close to us at times ask whether we're nervous when we face an important event in our life. And we naturally respond with "Of course not!" while having sweaty palms.

Nervousness physiologically is a crucial state because that's how the body is preparing itself for an extreme event. The sweaty palms, faster heartbeat, and narrowing concentration are all signs of a body in stress.

Taking the first step in the game shows a special type of courage, and by choosing an aggressive strategy, we force our opponents to respond to our initiative. We must jolt the adversary off balance, knowing that they're just as nervous as we are. Being the first to move also activates our fight-orflight instincts and relieves our anxiety that in extreme cases can cause complete paralysis.

HYDRATING BEFORE GAME

Sport drinks are a popular item in sports, but few people recognize their mental benefits.

For example, these types of drinks even work if the player only gets some in their mouth. In practice, the taste receptors in the mouth sense the sugar and signal the brain about the carbohydrate intake. In response, the brain stimulates the motor cortex and pleasure-sensing areas, thinking that it's soon getting some extra energy.

If we don't drink our entire bottle, we still get its effect without forcing our stomach to metabolize the extra load.

CHEER FOR SCORE

In most sports, it's quite obvious to see scoring by watching exclusively the suddenly cheering coach or the team. The exploding emotions are quite visible when a team scores a point. The long-term effect of expressed exuberance is that these players normally perform better after that and often lead their team to victory sooner as well.

This effect has been previously investigated in soccer (Moll, Jordet, & Pepping, 2010) and basketball (Kraus, Huang, & Keltner, 2010). In both cases, it's been found that outwardly displayed cheers and pronounced movements had a positive lasting effect on the winning side and a negative one on the losing team. For example, if the scoring team celebrated with both hands raised, there was twice the likelihood that the opposing team's players would miss scoring in a consequent penalty shot. Also, if a scoring player engaged more with their teammates following a successful shot, that player also tended to continue that streak.

DIFFERENCE BETWEEN WINNING AND WINNING

Winning is relative. If we think about the participating teams in a world championship, they quite likely already consider themselves winners, because they have already made it past all the possible eliminations to be there. Yet anything could happen at the finals and there will be only one ultimate champion.

> I don't want to win at all costs;
> I want us to be winners

When the final two teams are measured up against each other, they both go for the gold and wouldn't accept anything less besides being number one.

Still, the real winners aren't always who end up on top. Winning at all costs often is a cost too much to bear. Losing a game brings about a pang of disappointment but also the valuable time to reflect, which can later on result in positive changes. Those who consider a loss final will never arrive at winning in the future. This is what differentiates a winning character from a losing one: it can use the time of loss as a lesson, not a reason for self-pity.

Winning comes at the least expected time

Winners are made, not born. Every e-Athlete has their time eventually to be proud and glad for their achieved results. Joy is a part of sports and its happy moments are as important as its painful ones. Many e-Athletes talk about the mistakes made even after coming out on top and can't allow themselves to celebrate. This is misguided thinking, just as much as is viewing losses as permanent. It's important to put both winning and losing in their proper contexts.

Success is the joy in creation

Creativity is an essential part of winning. When something new and ingenious is inserted into a game, it gives it a new dimension and makes winning a particularly joyful event.

Participants of eSports are discoverers and stretch their own internal boundaries as much as the games'. Winning or losing, all players remember best their special moments of trying something new.

We should never shackle our minds with singular expectations about how only winning, medals, and monetary gains matter. Let's live through every round as if it were the most important and the only one we participate in. The experience becomes a whole only if we're giving our entire self to it.

11

CONNECTING WITH **FANS**

The next two chapters discuss topics not related to preparation for tournaments, but that are still integral parts of the world of eSports, and the consideration of which is a must for all teams.

The present chapter discusses the mental aspects of external communication for beginner and advanced teams.

ON INTERVIEWS

Developing connections with the media, fans, and supporters plays an important role in the life of an eSports team. In the case of a newly-formed team, this is usually free from hassles, since there is not much hype surrounding them.

However, in order to establish a beneficial everyday relationship between a professional team and the various organizations and media around them, the work should commence in the very beginning.

Regarding the quantity of interviews, extremes have to be avoided; thus, it is not advised to totally refrain from interviews nor is it to publish information on each and every team-related event.

Fans always turn to professional teams with some natural interest, to which it is worth reacting for the professional team, since a truly competitive team is supposed to set more goals than simply satisfying its own hunger for victory. Fans have a peculiar relationship with their team; special ties come into place after a while. The team and its players become the heroes of the fans; they can put themselves in their shoes during each match and thereby take part in their success.

WHAT TO FOCUS ON WHILE COMMUNICATING?

DIRECTNESS

Whether in an interview or a conversation, directness helps to build the bridge of communication. Fans shall not see team members as an unreachable player, but as someone who is one of them and belongs to them.

People tend to identify the most with those who stand the closest to them – speak the same language, fight for the same principles and goals, or behave as they do.

Directness helps players to leave the unnecessary masks behind and give the merits of their information to the fan or interviewer. This gives trust to the audience; they become more open towards the team.

WE ARE NOT BETTER

We might be the most successful eSports professionals in the world, but don't forget that **we are not better than any of our fans** who cross their fingers for us. The difference between an eSports player and a fan is that on a daily basis an eSports player spends more time competing and perfecting his play skills, while fans spend the same amount of time with other work or studies. Neither activity is better or worse than the other.

Since eSports players are in the center of attention during the games and events, and sometimes they are also recognized while in public, they tend to have the misconception of being more valuable than the ones who look upon them. However, if we stand in the shoes of a fan when one has to demonstrate his knowledge at a business meeting or a school exam, the player would feel the same as the fan feels while on the grandstand: cheering and wishing for good luck. **Greatness is relative and everyone's personality is equally valuable.**

TAKE THEM SERIOUSLY

Take seriously all of our conversations before an audience – this is as important as doing well during the tournaments.

However, there might be too interrogative a line of questions which is difficult or awkward to answer, or which we would like to evade; in such a case, just answer them briefly and simply. In contrast, there are questions pleasant to answer, to which we may give detailed answers and make the interviewer feel that this falls within our comfort zone.

The interviewer feels our seriousness from the meaningfulness and content of our answers. They instantly realize if someone gives evasive answers all the way, is distracted, or is not in the mood for the interview.

In order to take the interview seriously, we have to devote our time and attention.

TELL THE WHOLE STORY

Some questions at interviews pertain to a specific life situation or story. In this case, tell the whole story in your answer. The description of an actual life situation of a professional eSports player may be the most interesting part of an interview for the audience.

The story has to be told in sufficient detail, since details make it unique and special; tell what we felt at that moment, what mascot we had in our hands, tell anything that is related to us and our team. The more details we give, the more colorful the story becomes.

Storytelling gives life to the members of the team; mere names become credible persons. Feel free to use first names in our positive stories, since even those to whom the story points may read and feel happy from the interview.

Tell the story as if it would pertain to the audience, since even they would be able to join the team with sufficient exercise and motivation.

DON'T PROMISE VICTORY

As a sportsman, avoid promising victory in specific events or making other impossible promises. The purpose is to literally do our best at a match, but sometimes this is not enough for victory. Fans can be disappointed if we make irresponsible promises.

POSITIVE ENDING AT ALL TIMES

Sometimes we make mistakes; there is no shame in admitting them, since all of us are humans and everyone makes mistakes.

However, never end our train of thoughts with a negative comment. After admitting to our mistake, tell what we intend to change, what can be learnt from the mistakes, how to make capital out of the handicaps.

This changes our attitude as well as the attitude of the fans towards loss, and it will then be easier to learn from our negative experience.

RAISE EXPECTATIONS

Whether the interview takes place after a winning or a losing match, let's raise expectations in the fans upon the closing of the interview. Show them that we look forward to the next challenge, the next duty that lies before us. Raising hope is a key psychological factor, since it is uplifting for both the fans and the team players. For instance, think of how much more uplifting it is to construe and look forward to the forthcoming weekend's events on Monday than it is to recall the events of the past weekend.

CHANGING THE VIEW OF FANS

The view of fans seldom follows the actual performance of the team. For instance, let's compare the performance of an average team and the opinion of its fans match by match.

On the basis of its performance, the team is in the mid-range, but it is given an excellent coach at the beginning of the new season, who is dedicated to making a change in the life of the team.

The fans of the team are currently skeptical: they sometimes describe specific matches ironically even if they have been won by the team. However, everyone secretly hopes for improvement after years of variable performance.

The coach of the team starts his work, assesses the capabilities of the team, the quality of teamwork and communications, and then the actual training work begins.

The first competitive match ends up with an ignominious failure; old reactions re-appear without any trace of the new training after one month. The coach shakes the team together, then they continue the work. All in all, the supporting fans are disappointed after the match; they find that nothing has changed despite the young coach and the new arrangement.

In the second month, the team wins a competitive match in a tight fight with a seemingly easier competitor. The work of the team begins to be lightly perceivable, but they attribute the victory as a result of the team's own intrepidity. Although fans are happy for the victory, on the next day they rather state, on grounds of "reality", that the opponent gave them this victory.

Let's roll forward the wheel of time. One year has passed and the team starts to come together, the rehearsed configurations start to work, although the team still lacks the really easy victories. The last match of the season with an outstanding competitor ended up with a failure, although a year ago they would have anticipated the very same match with the doomed sense of the inevitable. The supporters sometimes recognize the development, but in fact they say that victory is victory and loss is loss.

After one year of hard work the team could not really change the opinion of the fans, no matter that the development became gradually and clearly perceivable for the team and the management.

In the next season, the team carried the day, won matches in landslide victory, even beat the champion team in a grandiose match, although only with one point.

By forgetting the earlier criticism, the fans celebrate the team as heroes; the supporters don't understand the reason for the success of the second year, nor what has changed things to such a great extent.

In fact, the real change occurred during the first year, and all results of the second year are rooted in the hard work of the first year.

12

LEADERS AND CAPTAINS

The present chapter is primarily addressed to the leaders, since their presence in the team is of outstanding significance and they can greatly take part in the success of the team. Nevertheless, the required skills and mental attitude are often unknown to them. What are the things to take care of, which characteristics are worth acquiring over time? Leaders are not born but made, and this requires development.

Leading an eSports team may itself be the road to becoming a leader. This chapter aims to provide guidance in this field.

ABOUT LEADERS FOR LEADERS

Each team begins with a leader who undertakes to organize a team and make a go of it.

Anyone who undertakes to do so must be prepared and persistent; this almost always pays off, since a good team is not just the sum of successes, but also an audience where the leader feels at home.

Leaders generally have the misconception that they are able to change the characteristics of people with their instructions, their authority, and thereby they are able to make them more effective. This is not true; as a parent and leader I know well that the **secret lies in setting a good example**. In addition, the change always needs the intention of the other party. The messages of the leaders or captains reach the players only in such a case.

Leadership is comprised of more than coordination and instructions. Leadership also means responsibility, which is carried on the back of the leader. If we often feel that our decisions haven't been adequate, or some situations could have been treated better otherwise, then we can ensure that we are capable of evolving as leaders.

WHAT MAKES A GOOD LEADER OUTSTANDING?

Starting after years-long experience, I collected the characteristics and personality traits which constitute a successful leader or captain. These characteristics result in a leader that is able to bring 110% out of his team.

I also strive to do exactly that as a leader, and I know that some points of the following list are difficult to achieve. Nonetheless, we must do our best to follow them.

1. A good leader is **always prepared** – whether it be a training day, the reviewing of match footage, or a simple meeting, he is always meaningful and determines the next step for the team
2. The leader is a **stable point** and consequent – the consistency and stability increases trust among the team members. People look upon those who they trust,

so if a leader devotes extra hours to a given task, then the members of the team will also devote extra hours to their own tasks over time

3. **Gives strict but honest feedback** – telling the harsh reality is unpleasant, but the team cannot progress while living under the illusion of false success and praise

4. **Says thanks** – when a member of the team does well, the good leader recognizes that in the long run saying thanks pays more than any amount of money could

5. **Listens to and cares for his team** – truth is always relative, and so the true coach learns from the members of the team, watches them, and listens to them, since the true leader cares for his team

6. **Unfolds his own vision** – excellent leaders are able to give the team a true vision in which they can fully believe

7. **Assigns tasks together with the underlying reasons** – whether it relates to training or competition, the adequate leader always tells the why of the task; there are always specific objectives behind seemingly odd tasks, and the team members have to be aware of these hidden objectives

8. The good leader is **together with his team** – they share a common locker, a common room

9. **Cannot be made angry** – even in the most critical situations

10. **Does not make judgments** – he gets closer to his team by understanding the problems and weaknesses of his team instead of making judgments

11. **Able to make decisions in all situations** – there are no situations where he cannot decide between option "A" and "B", since he knows that even a wrong decision is better than the lack of decision

12. **Guides into paths instead of building barriers** – Instead of continuously telling what is disallowed, he rather gives suggestions, directioris, in order to allow team members to use their creative energies properly

13. The true leader **does not follow the crowd** – he listens to his own opinion and intuitions even if the crowd speaks otherwise

HOW TO RECOGNIZE THE WORTHY LEADER

In 1959 Vince Lombardi became the coach of Green Bay Packers in the National Football League.

In one of his first speech to the team Lombardi said the following:

"Gentlemen, we are going to relentlessly chase perfection, knowing full well we will not catch it, because nothing is perfect. But we are going to relentlessly chase it, because in the process we will catch excellence. I am not remotely interested in just being good." (Havel, 2011)

Shortly after Lombardi's speech, Bart Starr called his wife Cherry and told her: were going to win lots of games.

"It was that obvious," sayd Starr. "That's what we were lacking when he came there: leadership." (Wojciechowski, 2006)

Many eSports players find the character of the leader important, for instance, when choosing their team, but how do you recognize the proper leader in the course of an interview or an informal meeting?

The following list gives hints in this regard.

- ☐ He **looks into your eyes** when talking to you
- ☐ He really **pays you attention** when you have something to say
- ☐ He speaks in first person plural, uses **"us"** instead of "me" or "you", (this reflects that he fights together with the team for one goal)
- ☐ He is **capable of smiling**, even if seldom doing so (this shows that he enjoys life)
- ☐ Instead of identifying with it, he **understands the problem**, since immersing into the problem would result in pulling himself down to the level of the problem instead of finding the solution
- ☐ The worthiness of the real leader is shown when he **does not feel he is better than any member of his team** (he is proud to work together with the team)
- ☐ He will be the **first to help the team** with his bare hands if needed (this reflects that he considers the team as first priority)

If we want to evolve as an eSports player, then choosing the proper leader is about as important as choosing our team members or in which game to compete. Relying on our first impression is the best thing that could help.

KEY THOUGHTS

(1) **Every goal wants to be reality**, almost as if they live their own life. — p. 11

(2) When a goal only exists in our mind, it does not come closer to reality. **We have to do physical steps in order to push our goals forward**. — p. 16

(3) **Our dreams will never become reality the same way we imagined them**. The realization is a creative process and we can't limit it. — p. 19

(4) **With intention, you are more likely to accomplish a goal** than with will. Intention searches for opportunities, will insists on something that is far away. — p. 24

(5) **Victory is the result of courage**; with fear in our hearts we can't win. — p. 25

(6) **Developing a skill, achieving a goal, is the result of hard work**, and there are no tricks or shortcuts. — p. 29

(7) **New abilities do not emerge gradually, they happen in leaps,** so for the first success you have to put a great amount of work in to achieve it. — p. 36

(8) **Never put negative things into positive message**, it works like poison. — p. 45

(9) **Humility appears among people who wish to develop.** They pay attention, but they don't accept

every thought as they hear it. They test them in the practice. — p. 68

(10) **Learning from our opponents** is one of the best ways to become as successful as they are. — p. 70

(11) To solve complex problems, money and intimidation are bad motivators. **Use praise or foster inner excellence instead.** — p. 85

(12) **Our outer self tends to get others' attention**, which works like energy, empowering the person. — p. 90

(13) **To establish harmony between our inner self and ego is mindfulness.** — p. 101

(14) The mirror effect helps to understand that **what we find annoying in others are the very things we avoid facing in ourselves**. — p. 103

(15) **In the state of being present, we experience a wider reality from our surrounding world**, events and happenings become more clear to us — p. 107

(16) **Primary intuition could be as wise as thoughtful deliberation**, because our subconscious deals with factors that would never appear on the surface of our conscious mind; this is why the first thought is in most cases the right one — p. 115

(17) **Our emotions are completely our creatures**, they are not related to any other — p. 125

(18) **Acceptance is a matter of conscious decision**; you can always choose the path that is right for you, even if it takes time to get there — p. 132

(19) **Our own opinion about our self is the only thing that matters**, if we listen to others we won't be able to

achieve great goals, because their thoughts will be limiting us — p. 150

(20) Thanks to **performance cycles** we can experience "everything works" moments even when we are not prepared for them. These **cycles help to make changes in our life**; it is important to deal with them— p. 153

REFERENCES

Berne, E. (1967). *Games people play: The psychology of human relationships.* Penguin UK.

Burch, N. (1970). *The Four Stages for Learning Any New Skill.* Retrieved from Gordon Training International: http://www.gordontraining.com/free-workplace-articles/learning-a-new-skill-is-easier-said-than-done/

Csikszentmihalyi, M. (1991). *Flow: The psychology of optimal experience.* HarperPerennial New York.

Glucksberg, S. (1962). The influence of strength of drive on functional fixedness and perceptual recognition. *Journal of Experimental Psychology, 63*(1), 36.

Havel, C. (2011). *Lombardi - An Illustrated Life.* Krause Publications.

Hobson, J., Pace-Schott, E., & Stickgold, R. (2000). Dreaming and the brain: toward a cognitive neuroscience of conscious states. *Behavioral and Brain Sciences, 23*, 793-842.

Kraus, M. W., Huang, C., & Keltner, D. (2010). Tactile communication, cooperation, and performance: an ethological study of the NBA. *Emotion, 10*(5), 745.

REFERENCES

Kübler-Ross, E. (2009). *On death and dying: What the dying have to teach doctors, nurses, clergy and their own families.* Taylor & Francis.

Lally, P., Van Jaarsveld, C., Potts, H., & Wardle, J. (2010). How are habits formed: Modelling habit formation in the real world. *European Journal of Social Psychology, 40*(6), 998-1009.

Ledgerwood, A., & E. Boydstun, A. (2014). Sticky Prospects: Loss Frames Are Cognitively Stickier Than Gain Frames. *Journal of Experimental Psychology: General, 143*(1), 376.

McDowall, M. (Director). (2011). *Ronaldo: Tested to the Limit* [Motion Picture].

Moll, T., Jordet, G., & Pepping, G.-J. (2010). Emotional contagion in soccer penalty shootouts: Celebration of individual success is associated with ultimate team success. *Journal of sports sciences, 28*(9), 983-992.

Most, S., Simons, D., Scholl, B., & Chabris, C. (2000). Sustained inattentional blindness. *Psyche, 6*(14).

Murray, H. A. (1938). *Explorations in personality.* Oxford University Press.

Robert, M., & Thomas, J. (1990, January 11). Johnny Sylvester, the Inspiration For Babe Ruth Heroics, Is Dead. *The New York Times*. Retrieved from http://www.nytimes.com/1990/01/11/obituaries/joh nny-sylvester-the-inspiration-for-babe-ruth-heroics- is-dead.html

Vogel, M. (2012, June 5). Prep runner carries foe to finish line. (D. Binder, Interviewer)

Wegner, D., Schneider, D., Carter, S., & White, T. (1987). Paradoxical effects of thought suppression. *Journal of personality and social psychology, 53*(1), 5.

Wojciechowski, G. (2006, February 4). *Lombardi turned Packers into winners*. Retrieved from ESPN: http://www.espn.com/espn/columns/story?columnist=wojciechowski_gene&id=2318158

Books are valuable only in hands

If you enjoyed reading this book or you found some
important messages in it,
don't hesitate to give it to your friend.

(The Author)

Made in the USA
Monee, IL
09 July 2022